STAINED GLASS
IN ENGLAND : 1150-1550

STAINED GLASS
IN ENGLAND: 1150-1550

Brian Coe FRSA

W. H. Allen · London
A Howard & Wyndham Company
1981

Printed and bound in Great Britain
by W. S. Cowell Ltd., Ipswich
for the publishers W. H. Allen & Co. Ltd.,
44 Hill Street, London W1X 8LB.

ISBN 0 491 02794 X

Design by Mary Spendlove

CONTENTS

ILLUSTRATIONS

Colour

Half-tone

FOREWORD

I welcome this enlightened and well-informed book. When I was nineteen or twenty I began to try to study the *art* of English medieval stained glass but there was little to be found in the way of published work. Books about the *craft* existed all right, and for the whereabouts of glass there was Dr Nelson's *Ancient Painted Glass in England* (1913 – not wholly complete nor wholly reliable) mentioned by Mr Coe in his bibliography. Otherwise, one could scuffle through Methuen's *Little Guides* to individual counties, or Murray's Handbooks, or the few volumes of the *Victoria County History* then existing. Adequate illustrations were extremely rare. Much less has happened since the early 1920s to alter this situation than one might think. Herbert Read's *English Stained Glass*, 1926, showed – almost for the first time in Great Britain – that stained glass was art, or could be so; not just craft. Baker and Lammer's book of 1960 has fine, coloured illustrations, and the glass in a few particular churches (Canterbury, York, Malvern) and a few special areas has been well dealt with in an archaeological way. And of course there is Pevsner to thumb through. But there is plenty of room for this book, and I find myself delighted by the splendour of the colour photography, by the care of the author's topographical research and by the open-mindedness of his whole approach. I hope his work will stimulate Deans of cathedrals and incumbents of churches in the production of more and better reproductions, posters, books and postcards of English stained glass – enough to compare with the generous number of good quality sold in so many churches on the Continent.

JOHN PIPER

INTRODUCTION

WHETHER as a regular churchgoer or just a casual visitor, everyone is likely to be familiar with the effect of sunlight streaming through a richly coloured stained-glass window. Few take the trouble to look closely at the windows, which can tell us so much about the past. The churches of England contain a great deal of glass made in the last hundred and fifty years, some of it of excellent quality, but much of it dull and uninspired. Here and there a panel, or even a whole window, will stand out in its richness of colour and strength of line. There is a good chance that this glass will date from the Middle Ages, from which a surprising quantity of glass survives. The aim of this book is to introduce to the reader the story of medieval stained glass, to explain how the windows were made, who made them, how the different styles of the various periods may be identified and to describe the subjects that they may depict. To help the enthusiast find old glass, a selective county guide is included. It must be emphasised that this is a subject complex in all its aspects, and for more detailed study the literature listed in the bibliography must be consulted.

In this book the popular, if not entirely exact, term 'stained glass' will be used to describe the finished window. Glass may be stained or coloured during manufacture, but during the making of the window details would be painted upon each piece of glass. For this reason, some authorities prefer to call the medium painted glass, or stained and painted glass. The latter term is too cumbersome, and the former no more exact. 'Stained glass' will be taken to refer to all the techniques used in the preparation of a window.

Most of the early glass remaining in the British Isles is to be found in England. Only negligible amounts survive in Scotland, and in Wales there are only a few churches with any quantity of medieval glass. The author requests the indulgence of Scots and Welsh friends if, in referring to English stained glass, any to be found in their countries is included. During the late eighteenth and nineteenth centuries large quantities of stained glass were brought to this country from Europe and installed in churches. Such glass, although not of English origin, is included in this survey, since it may often provide instructive comparisons with glass of the same period but of local manufacture.

Where place names are given, they should be taken to refer to the parish church of the locale concerned. They should not be taken as the only places where the subjects or techniques under discussion may be found, but as representative only. A glossary is provided as a source of rapid reference to some of the architectural and other terms not explained in the text.

1

HOW A WINDOW WAS MADE

THE origins of the craft of stained-glass window making are obscure. Glass, the manufacture of which was known to the Egyptians five thousand years ago, was used by the Romans for window glazing, especially in their northern territories where the climate made it more necessary. Fragments of flat glass have been found at sites in Britain, and larger slabs were discovered in excavations at Pompeii and Herculaneum. We know that glass was set in metal frames, including some of lead, by the Romans, but there is no reason to believe that these early windows were anything more than simple mosaics of unpainted glass. From the writings of the Venerable Bede, we learn that French glaziers were brought over to work on the churches of Jarrow and Wearmouth around the year 680. Again, we may assume that this was plain glazing, at best arranged in simple decorative patterns. It is generally believed that the medium of stained glass was considerably influenced by the techniques of enamelling introduced from Byzantium into France about 972. In particular, the *cloisonné* method involved soldering copper or brass wire, bent to a suitable design, onto a similar ground; the compartments so formed were then filled with enamels of different colours. By firing in a kiln or furnace, the enamels were bonded to the metal, producing a mosaic of colours, each separated from its neighbour by a thin metallic line. The close similarity of this structure to that of the transparent glass window – a mosaic of coloured glass held together with lead strips – is obvious.

Near the end of the tenth century techniques were developed for painting details of faces, drapery, ornament etc. onto the glass and by the middle of the eleventh century glass painting had clearly become a well-established technique. Pictorial stained glass believed to date from the ninth century can be seen in Lorsch Abbey, Germany, while Le Mans Cathedral in France has glass of *c.* 1090 in which the techniques are quite accomplished. It appears that by 1134 glaziers were producing windows of such remarkable decoration that the austere Cistercian order issued an edict requiring glazing to be restricted to the use of white glass only. The methods in use at this time for the manufacture of the glass, its preparation and assembly have remained almost unchanged to the present day.

The first detailed account of the methods of manufacture was given by an artist and monk, Theophilus, in a three-volume treatise on art, *Diversarum Artium Schedula*. The first volume described techniques of painting, the second the manufacture and painting of glass and the third dealt with metal-working. The exact date of the work is not clear; it may have been written as early as the eleventh century, but was more probably of the twelfth. Since Theophilus's aim was to give precise instructions to the would-be glassmaker, it is worth quoting from his book at length. First he explained how to construct a furnace from stones and clay, and how to make ash by burning dried beech-wood. Usually this was carried out in an iron pot, producing pot-ash. Then came the instructions for making the glass:

> Then taking two parts of the ashes . . . and a third of sand, carefully purified from earth and stones, which sand you shall have taken out of water, mix them together in a clean place. And when they have been for a long time and well mixed together, taking them up with an iron trowel, put them in the smaller part of the furnace, upon the upper hearth that they may be roasted: and when they have begun to grow hot, immediately stir them, lest they chance to melt by the heat of the fire and run into balls. Do this for the space of a day and a night.

The mass of roasted but not fused material, called 'frit' by the glassmaker, was melted when needed in clay pots, over a whole night, until it was completely melted, or 'fluxed'. All was then ready to make sheets of glass.

> . . . take an iron tube, and . . . put the extremity of it into a pot filled with glass: when the glass adheres to it turn the tube in your hand until there is conglomerated round it as much as you want. Then draw it out, put it to your mouth and blow gently . . . You should have a flat stone before the window [of the furnace], on which you will gently beat the hot glass, that it may hang equally on every side . . . When you perceive that the glass hangs like a long bladder, hold its extremity in the flame, and the end immediately becoming melted a hole will be visible in it. Take a piece of wood formed for this purpose, and make the hole as large as [the bladder of glass] is in the middle, then join its lips together . . . so that on either side of the juncture an opening may be visible. Immediately touch the glass near the tube with a piece of moist wood, shake it a little, and it will separate [from the tube]. Then heat the tube . . . until the glass which adheres to it melts, and quickly put it to the two lips of the glass which have been joined, and it will adhere to them . . . put it in the flame of the furnace until the hole from which you first separated the tube melts. Take a round piece of wood, and widen this hole as you did the other. And wrapping the edges of the glass together in the middle, separate the glass from the tube with a piece of moist wood . . .

The cylinders so formed were taken and stored in an annealing furnace of moderate temperature. When the whole of the original mix had been converted to cylinders it was time to make them into sheets.

> . . . take a hot iron, and having split one side of the glass [cylinder] lay it on the hearth of the heated furnace, and when it begins to soften, take the iron tongs and a smooth piece of wood, and opening it in that part in which it is split, spread it out, and flatten it at pleasure with the tongs.

The sheets or 'tables' of glass were allowed to cool in the annealing furnace. This method, known as the 'muff' process, could be used to make sheets of uneven thickness of around twenty-four inches by fifteen. Sheet glass made in this way can be identified by the presence of bubbles running in parallel lines. An alternative method of manufacture began by blowing a large bubble of glass on an iron tube, as before. The bubble was then transferred to a heated iron rod, and the hole created by the removal of the pipe was opened out by rapidly rotating the rod. Spinning rapidly, the bubble was transformed into a disc of as much as twenty-four inches in diameter. After being removed from the rod, the disc was annealed as before. At the centre of the disc was a thick boss where the rod was attached; this part was used for the 'bull's-eye' glazing of domestic windows. Glass produced in this way is known as 'crown', and the bubbles in it run in concentric circles.

The molten glass, known as 'pot-metal', could be coloured by the addition of metallic oxides to the mix. Copper oxide gave a deep ruby-red glass, iron oxide gave green, cobalt oxide blue, manganese oxide purple and sulphur or soot gave yellow. The oxide-bearing earths used in medieval times contained many impurities, and gave a wide range of colour variation. Frequently, what was intended to be white glass ended up coloured, through impurities in the sand or ash. Theophilus suggested how this might be exploited:

> If indeed you observe that [the glass in] any pot happens to change to a tan colour which is like flesh, keep this glass for flesh colour; and taking as much of it as you want, fuse the residue for two hours . . . and you will have a light purple. And again fuse it from the third to the sixth hour, and it will be a red and perfect purple.

Although richly coloured, these glasses allowed plenty of light to pass, except for the red glass made by adding copper oxide. Here the colour was so dense as to be almost black, unless it was made in sheets too thin and fragile to be satisfactory. Early on, a technique known as 'flashing' was introduced: the glass-maker first took a bubble of red glass on his blowpipe, then dipped it several times into a pot of molten white glass. The mass was blown as before, to give a sheet of white glass with a thin flashing or coating of red. The white glass provided a strong support for the layer of brilliant colour. Early flashed glass was often streaky, but this defect could be turned to advantage by the glazier, to give an effect of texture, wood grain and so on in a picture. An interesting example is in a thirteenth-century window of the Trinity Chapel in Canterbury Cathedral. A carpenter is shown cutting his leg with an axe. The axe blade is of white glass, with a streak of ruby to represent blood. A Crucifixion panel of around 1245 at Twycross, Leicestershire, shows streaky-red glass used for the Cross, with a distinct effect of graining. Careful study of early windows will reveal many examples of this effective use of what was, theoretically, spoiled glass. From around the end of the fifteenth century, blue glass was also made by coating in this way.

Before the sixteenth century, virtually all coloured glass used in Britain was imported from two main centres on the Continent. Rhenish glass, from Hesse and Lorraine, was usually brought in through the northern ports, while French glass, from Normandy and Lower Burgundy, came in through the south. During the four hundred years we are considering manufacturing methods improved, and the thick, uneven glass of the earliest period gradually became smoother, clearer and thinner.

Equipped with a suitable stock of white and coloured glass, the glazier could begin. First, a design was prepared, based upon the customer's requirements. The method used in the earlier period was, again, described by Theophilus:

> When you desire to construct glass windows, first make yourself a smooth wooden board of such length and breadth that you can work on it two panels of each windows. Then take chalk, and scraping it with a knife over the whole table, sprinkle water thereon in every part, and rub the table entirely over with a cloth. When it is dry, take measure of the length and breadth of one panel of the window, describe it on the table by rule and compass, with lead, or tin [used as a pencil]. If you wish to have a border in it, draw it of such a breadth as pleases you, and with such workmanship as you wish. This done, draw as many figures as you like, first with lead, or tin, then in the same manner with a red or black colour, making all the strokes carefully, because it will be necessary when you shall have painted the glass to join the shadows and lights

Heads from the same cartoon, reversed, *c.* 1305 – Lady Chapel, Wells Cathedral, Somerset

according to the board. Then arrange the various draperies, and mark down the colour of each in its place . . . with a letter.

The use of whitewashed boards for designing windows gave way to the preparation of 'cartoons' on paper, around the middle of the fourteenth century. These had the great advantage that they could be reused, and they were, frequently.

[4]

'St Christopher' drawn from the same cartoon; *left :* First half of the fifteenth century – All Saints, North Street, York; *right : c.* 1535 – St Michael le Belfry, York

Series of figures of saints, destined for the tops of windows, could be painted from one cartoon, identical to each other except for a changed emblem, or differences of colour. Sometimes designs were simply reversed laterally. Examples of figures painted from the same cartoon can be seen in the fifteenth-century glass at North Cadbury, Somerset; in glass of 1470 at North Cerney, Gloucestershire; in the fourteenth-century glass in the Lady Chapel at Wells Cathedral and in the east window at East Harling church, Norfolk, where the design for the scene of the Ascension has been reversed and used for the Pentecost panel, with the descending Dove replacing the ascending feet of Christ.

Two representations of Saint Christopher, in All Saints, North Street, and Saint Michael le Belfrey churches in York appear to be from the same cartoon.

The remarkable thing is that the former was made in the first half of the fifteenth century and the second was painted around 1535. The cartoon must have passed from hand to hand for a hundred years. Other examples of the re-use of cartoons may be found throughout the country. These short-cuts for the glazier conflict with the sentimental view of medieval craftsman held by some Victorian writers. Their theory that the artist-craftsman put his finest work where only God could see it is not borne out by the often indifferent quality of the more remote glass. Then, as now, the customer got what he paid for. Original designs, in high-quality glass, cost much more than standard patterns made from inferior glass and sold by the square foot.

When the design on board or paper was complete, the glass could be cut. Theophilus recommended marking the glass before cutting it:

> . . . take a small leaden vessel, and put in it chalk pounded with water; make yourself two or three hair pencils, viz., of the tail of a martin, or ermine, or squirrel, or cat, or of an ass's mane. Take a piece of glass . . . which must be in every way larger than the place it is to occupy, and lay it flat on this place. When you have seen the strokes on the board through the glass, draw with the chalk upon the glass the outer strokes only . . . Afterwards, heat in the fire the dividing iron, which should be thin in every part, but thicker at the extremity [like a modern soldering iron]. When it is red hot in the thickest part, apply it to the glass which you wish to divide, and soon the beginning of a crack will appear. If the glass should be hard, moisten it with saliva with your finger in the place where you had applied the iron. As soon as it is cracked, draw the iron in the direction in which you wish to divide the glass, and the crack will follow the iron. All the pieces having been thus divided, take the grosing iron, which should be a palm long, and bent back at each end, with which you can smoothen and fit together all the pieces, each in its place.

The grosing iron was a strip of metal with a hooked or notched end, used, like the notched end of a modern glasscutter, to nibble away at the edge of the glass until it was the required shape. Grosing irons are represented in heraldic glass at St Helen's, York, and Sherborne Abbey, Dorset. The use of diamonds for glass cutting is quite recent, and the very clean edge given by this method enables the restorer to distinguish modern insertions from original glass when it is taken from the leads. Despite the apparent crudity of his tools, the medieval glazier could cut quite intricate shapes. A good example can be seen in an early-thirteenth-century panel in Canterbury Cathedral's Trinity Chapel, where the cellarer of Jervaulx Abbey is miraculously cured by a discharge of blood. The narrow, wavy strip of red glass must have represented a real challenge to the glazier, and it would not be an easy proposition even today.

With the glass cut to shape and laid out on the board or cartoon, the details of the design were added. This was done in 'enamel' prepared by the glazier. Theophilus's formula was:

> Take copper, beaten small, and burn it in a small iron pipkin until it is entirely pulverised. Then take pieces of green glass and Greek sapphire and pound them separately between two porphyry stones. Mix the three ingredients together in the proportions of one third powder, one third green glass and one third sapphire. Pound them together on the same stone with wine or urine very carefully, put them into an iron, or leaded, vessel, and paint the glass with the utmost care, according to the strokes that are upon the board. If you wish to make letters on the glass, you will cover those parts of the glass entirely with the same colour, and write the letters with the handle of the brush.

Opposite : Two grosing irons shown in a fragment of heraldic glass at Sherborne Abbey, Dorset; *below :* 'Hugh the Cellarer Cured by a Discharge of Blood' – a detail from a panel of *c.* 1220, showing an intricate shape which must have presented difficulty for the medieval glazier – Trinity Chapel, Canterbury Cathedral

This combination of metallic oxide and soft glass as a flux remained in use throughout the medieval period. The enamel was painted on with brushes of hog or badger hair, and the end of the brush handle could be used to remove the enamel where necessary, as Theophilus suggested. When all the details of faces, drapery and so on had been painted, the glass pieces were laid out on trays covered with lime and fired in a form of kiln, in which the enamel melted and fused to the surface of the glass.

When the glass was cool it was ready for assembly, and once again returned to the worktable. Grooved lead strips, with an H shape in cross-section were used. As with all the other necessary processes, Theophilus gave details of manufacture:

> Make yourself two irons two fingers broad, one finger thick and an ell long. Join them at one extremity like a hinge, in order that they may keep together, being fastened by a nail, so as to be able to open and shut. At the other extremity make them a little broader and thinner, so that when they are shut together, there may be, as it were, the beginning of a hollow within. Let the outer sides be parallel, and you should so fit the irons to each other . . . that no light shall appear between them. After this, separate them from each other, and taking a rule, make in the middle of one of them two lines, and opposite, two lines in the middle of the other, from top to bottom, of little width. Hollow these [lines] out with the tool used for hollowing . . . cast metal works, as deeply as you wish. In each iron scrape a little between the lines . . . in order that when you pour the lead into them, it may form only one piece.

The pieces of coloured and painted glass are held together by soldered lead strips. Fifteenth century, Norwich school – Ashill, Norfolk

The hollowed-out grooves formed the edges or leaves of the lead strips, and the scraped-out parts, the central supporting core, when molten lead was poured into the mould. The leads were called calmes, possibly from the Latin *calamus*, a hollow reed, and perhaps a reference to the mould in which they were cast. Theophilus also described the making of a simpler wooden mould in which lead rods could be cast. These could be cut and scraped on two sides to make the calmes. In addition to these grooved lead strips, solder was needed, made in rods cast from a mixture of five parts of tin with one part of lead.

With the painted glass, leads and solder prepared, the assembly of the window could begin. The first piece of glass was taken up and carefully surrounded by a strip of lead, bent to follow the outline closely. The piece was then returned to the table and temporarily fixed in position with 'closing' nails. An adjacent piece of glass was taken, leaded and replaced next to the first, and so on. Where the leads met, they were soldered carefully, using a heated iron and wax or suet as a flux. As new pieces were added and soldered, the closing nails were removed and re-used. When the whole panel was assembled it was turned over and the joints soldered on the reverse. Cement was then rubbed into the cracks between lead and glass to make a waterproof seal, and lead strips or copper wires were soldered at suitable points as ties to fix the panel to the supporting bars set in the window masonry. The early narrow lancet windows required only crossbars, called sondlets; wider windows needed a grid of horizontal and vertical bars, the latter called standings or stanchions. In the late twelfth and early thirteenth centuries this ironwork was sometimes bent to follow the pattern of medallion panels popular at the time. The windows of the Trinity Chapel in Canterbury Cathedral show this shaped ironwork, especially obvious where plain glass has replaced the original.

The earliest windows were constructed like a mosaic, the pieces of glass being small, each of a single colour. Like the enamels they resembled, the stained-glass windows required the intervention of a metal strip wherever there was to be a change of colour. These lead lines formed the main feature of the design, so much so that from the outside the general nature of the subject represented can be recognised easily in the early glass. This was not so in the later fourteenth and fifteenth centuries. Enamel painting was used in the early windows to give only the detail and shading of the picture. The rule – one colour to each piece of glass – applied to all early windows, except where, perhaps, a piece of 'spoiled' ruby glass might be used to give red and white, as already discussed.

The first break from this principle occurred early in the fourteenth century. An unknown glazier discovered that silver compounds, usually silver oxide or silver chloride, if applied in solution to white glass and fired in the kiln, gave an indelible yellow stain. Legend has it that it was a silver button, falling accidently into a glass kiln, that gave the clue. However the discovery came about, the silver staining process provided the glazier with a valuable new technique. No longer was a clumsy lead line needed between the white glass face and pot-metal yellow hair of a figure. Now the hair could be painted in silver stain on the same piece of glass as the face. Variations in the staining process could be used to give a range of colour from pale lemon-yellow to deep orange, distinctly different from the pot-metal yellow. The method appears to have been introduced around 1306 and was in widespread use by 1320.

A later development allowing colour variations on one piece of glass came into general use around the middle of the fifteenth century. Glaziers found that by abrading the red coating on white glass to reveal the underlying white, patterns of white on red, or red on white, could be made without intervening lead lines. This technique was especially useful in heraldic glass, where the very fine detail of the charges could not be displayed easily when cumbersome leads were needed. A good example of the solution to this problem can be seen in the late-fifteenth-century glass at Long Melford, Suffolk, in a remarkable series of figures of the Clopton family and associates. Two ladies of the Howard family are in heraldic mantles, displaying a design of crosses 'botonée fitchée' in white on red. In one panel, the crosses are painted out with enamel on small pieces of glass, leaded into red glass in a rather clumsy fashion. In the other, the crosses have been neatly abraded through flashed ruby glass. Another example can be seen at Bale, Norfolk, where the robe of the Virgin has an intricate 'M' monogram in abraded ruby glass. Silver staining could be applied to the white glass uncovered by abrasion, so that red, yellow and white could be shown on one piece of glass. Examples of combined abrasion and silver staining can be found at Margaretting, Essex (on the robe of Jesse in the east window), Fairford, Gloucestershire (in many windows), and on heraldic tabards on figures of Sir Robert Clifford at Long Melford and Richard Beaumont, Earl of Warwick, at Warwick, St Mary. By the end of the fifteenth century the same technique of abrasion was being applied to flashed blue glass, a good example being shown in an heraldic panel at St Winnow, Cornwall, where rampant lions have been neatly abraded from the blue coating. At Bolton Percy, Yorkshire, figures carry books represented by abraded blue and ruby glass.

Yet another variation of colour could be produced by applying silver stain to pale-coloured glass to vary the colour of details. For example, in a fifteenth-century panel of Saint Anne and the Virgin, at Almondbury, Yorkshire, silver stain has been used on pale-blue glass to colour a flower pattern green.

Although these methods of increasing the variety of colour had advantages for the glazier, they carried in them the seeds of destruction of the purity of the art and craft of stained-glass window making. Improvements in the manufacture of glass made possible larger sheets of greater evenness, encouraging a move away

[9]

Below : The technique of abrading flashed ruby glass used to produce a heraldic motif, compared with, *abov* the traditional leading-in method. Fifteenth century, Norwich school – Long Melford, Suffolk

from the effect of a mosaic of brilliant, small, coloured fragments characteristic of the earlier glass. By 1500 there were clear signs of a degeneration of technique. Rather than resort to the tedious, if effective, assembly of small pieces of glass, the glazier began to use larger sheets of white glass, on which the picture was painted in enamel and silver stain, using separate pieces of coloured glass only where vital. The lead lines ceased to play a significant part in the design, surviving only as mere mechanical links. As a result, the later windows often lack the clarity of line of the earlier examples. In the middle of the sixteenth century worse was to happen. It was discovered that coloured enamels could be made by grinding up coloured glass with a suitable flux. Painting on glass, as a painter applied colours to a canvas, the glazier could use his enamels to produce a whole design on a single sheet of glass. When fired in a kiln, the coloured enamels bonded to the glass, but tended to be pale when compared with those of the pot-metal. The adhesion of the enamels was often imperfect, and a disastrous tendency to flake off resulted in the 'moth-eaten' appearance of many surviving enamels. The method was cheap and quick, however, and much used for domestic glazing, especially in Switzerland in the sixteenth and seventeenth centuries.

The production of stained glass in England in the sixteenth century, already in artistic decline, as the departure from the Gothic tradition was not adequately offset by the influence of the Renaissance, came to an abrupt halt with the Reformation. Henry VIII's Injunctions of 1536 and 1538, suppressing the monasteries, together with Edward VI's Royal Articles of 1547, encouraged the wholesale destruction of 'idolatrous' images. Article 28 of 1547 commanded that '. . . they shall take away, utterly extinct and destroy all shrines, coverings of shrines, all tables, candlesticks, trindles or rolls of wax, pictures, paintings, and all other monuments of feigned miracles, pilgrimages, idolatry, and superstition; so that there remain no memory of the same in walls, glass-windows or elsewhere in their churches or houses.' With such a decree in force, there was clearly no market for new windows in churches. Glaziers were still employed to take out the glass and replace it with plain glazing, and were able to follow their craft by supplying the growing demand for heraldic glass for domestic windows.

It was not just a question of there being no new commissions for church windows. There was an active campaign of destruction set off by the Royal edicts. Of course, much early glass had already been destroyed to make way for new windows. The richer the parish, the more likely it was that old glass had been cleared away during the great wave of rebuilding in the fifteenth century. This was particularly true in areas where the wool trade flourished; Norfolk is typical of a county rich in fifteenth-century glass, but with little of earlier periods. The fragile windows were always at risk: if not properly maintained, they could be blown in by high winds. In addition, they suffered from the attentions of the young with arrows or balls. In the early fifteenth century the Bishop of London publicly criticised the ball-players whose games had broken windows in Old Saint Paul's Cathedral. But systematic destruction was something new. First, the monastic churches were demolished or stripped and left to decay. With them were destroyed enormous quantities of stained glass. Because of certain uncomfortable parallels between his situation and that of Henry II, Henry VIII ordered the removal of all images of Thomas à Becket from churches throughout the country. This operation was so successful that only a handful of representations of this most popular English saint survive, although once almost every church might be expected to have had one. In the reigns of Edward VI and Elizabeth I a similar campaign was mounted to remove figures of the Virgin Mary. The enthusiasm which developed for the destruction of idolatrous images soon got out of hand, and had to be curbed on purely practical grounds. A proclamation early in the reign of Elizabeth forbade the destruction of church windows without express permission, on pain of imprisonment.

A brief revival of interest in glass-painting in the early seventeenth century was soon ended by the upheaval of the Civil War. In 1640 a new campaign against idolatry began with a greater vigour than ever before. The dreaded William Dowsing, a Parliamentary Visitor, in 1643 and 1644 smashed his way through East Anglia, destroying windows and church ornaments ruthlessly. He kept a detailed record of his activities ". . . Sudbury . . . Gregory Parish, January 9th. We brake down 10 mighty great Angels in glass, in all 80 . . . Stoke Nayland, Jan. the 19th. We brake down an 100 superstitious pictures . . . Eye, Aug. the 30th. Seven superstitious pictures in the Chancel, and a cross; one was Mary Magdalene; all in the glass; and six in the church windows . . .".

Puritan ministers took it upon themselves to destroy religious imagery; Richard Culmer, Rector of Chartham in Kent, reported how he and a group of Puritan fanatics knocked out many of the windows of Canterbury Cathedral; one minister, with a pike, using a long ladder to reach the higher glass, occupied himself 'rattling down proud Becket's glassy bones'. Canon Jenkinson of Christ Church, Oxford, is said to have 'furiously stamped upon the windows of his cathedral when taken down, utterly defacing them'. In a bizarre episode at Winchester, soldiers used the bones of Saxon kings to throw at and smash the glass. Fortunately for us, in many places religious zeal was satisfied by removing only the heads of saints or figures of Christ, which were especially singled out for destruction.

Some glass was saved by removal for safe keeping. A notable example is the beautiful east window of East Harling church, Norfolk, which escaped destruction by Dowsing and his colleagues by being hidden during the Commonwealth, and was restored to the church in 1736. Even there, the heads of several of the representations of Christ are not original. The glass at Fairford, Gloucestershire, is said to have been removed for safe keeping, while the survival of so much glass in the churches of the city of York is due to the acceptance by Lord Fairfax, besieging the city, of the preservation of the glass and other furnishings as a condition of surrender.

Unhappily, the tale of destruction does not end with the restoration of more stable times. Ancient windows were replaced by eighteenth-century glass of indifferent quality. The most disastrous example of this was in the restoration of Salisbury Cathedral in 1788, when most of the old glass was stripped out and thrown into the town ditch, after the lead was removed. Windows were simply left to decay through lack of repair or maintenance. Such windows were prone to damage by storms or winds, as happened at Fairford, where the west windows of the aisles were blown in during a great storm in 1703. The glass at Combs, Suffolk, was damaged by an explosion at the nearby Stowmarket gunpowder mills in 1871.

In other places, windows were removed from churches to private collections, or were donated to other churches. The revival of interest in stained glass in the nineteenth century led to more removal of old glass to make way for new, but often inferior, windows. In some places glass-painters were commissioned to restore ancient glass, but made copies which were placed in the church and the original glass disposed of, often by private sale. An example was the late-twelfth-century Jesse Tree window in the Corona of Canterbury Cathedral, two panels of which were replaced during restoration; they were returned to the Cathedral in 1954. The upper half of the west window at Fairford, Gloucestershire, was copied by the early Victorian restorers and the old glass was disposed of or destroyed. Even where the old glass might be retained in a church, it was often removed from its original setting to another, frequently inappropriate, location, a process which, unhappily, still continues. Pieces of glass from several locations within a church might be leaded up together in a meaningless jumble, from which there is little hope of making sense of the original scheme. Even in these enlightened times the record is not always satisfactory. In some places, glass removed for safe keeping during the Second World War has been put back with the painted side out, accelerating the loss of detail through weathering. A lesser, but still unfortunate, offence is the practice of placing panels of dark, richly coloured old glass in a window of plain white glass, the glare from which makes appreciation of detail and colour difficult. Sometimes, windows of old glass are assembled with modern glass of incompatible hues. A sad example of this is at Twycross, Leicestershire, where priceless panels of twelfth- and thirteenth-century glass from France have been surrounded with borders of yellow and purple glass quite out of keeping with it.

On the other hand, much recent restoration has been carried out with great care and skill. Careful rearrangement of many jumbled fragments has revealed something of the original scheme. An impressive example can be seen at All Saints, North Street, York, where until recently a south aisle window was a collection of miscellaneous fragments. With the aid of centuries-old sketches, the restorer has reassembled the glass into a recognisable representation of a Corpus Christi procession. The task confronting the restorer in such a case can be better understood by imagining the problems of assembling a jigsaw-puzzle picture from a box of mixed pieces from a number of puzzles, with a large number removed, and without an accurate picture as a guide.

It is important to remember that all surviving medieval glass has been releaded many times, and restored to some extent. Rarely, the restoration has been limited to releading and repair of broken pieces; more often, new glass has been added, or old scraps brought from elsewhere have been used to fill up gaps. In the wave of restoration during the Gothic revival in the last century, remains of old glass were often incorporated in new windows, which more or less faithfully followed the original scheme. The many examples include the Jesse Tree in the east window of Selby Abbey, about half of which is original glass, another Jesse Tree at Leverington, Cambridgeshire, where only thirteen of the sixty-one figures are completely original, and the east window at Elland, Yorkshire, in which only eight of the twenty-one panels are mostly of the fifteenth century. At Himbleton, Worcestershire, a modern window in the style of 1300 has a single original figure. Sometimes, restoration is limited to replacing heads, notably of Christ, destroyed in earlier times. Frequently, the replacements have been drawn in such a way as to stand out all too obviously. The upper part of the figure of Christ in several panels at East Harling, Norfolk, is seen clearly to be restoration when compared with original representations in other panels in the same window. Similarly, the faces of the four sons of Ralph Neville, in the very restored fourteenth-century glass at Well, Yorkshire, have a wrong look to them. The figure of Christ in the Seven Sacraments window at Doddiscombleigh, Devon, is completely modern, and quite out of keeping with the fifteenth-century glass which surrounds it.

The repair of broken glass often results in an obtrusive lead line obscuring detail of a face. 'Plating', the sandwiching of the broken pieces between two pieces of thin, plain glass cut to shape, overcomes this problem. It was used with great success in the restoration of the 'Acts of Mercy' window in All Saints, North Street, York,

Details of the Acts of Mercy window at All Saints, North Street, York; *above*: before cleaning and repair; *below*: after cleaning and 'plating' of damaged glass.
Opposite above, left: The characteristic silvery appearance of old glass, seen from outside – Swinbrook, Oxfordshire; *above, right*: The etched surface of early glass – Stottesdon, Shropshire; *below*: a magnified view of the pits etched into the glass by weathering and pollution – Stratton on the Fosse, Somerset

in 1965. Obscuring leads were removed, to the great advantage of the window; the thin cracks in the glass are now much less obtrusive.

There are other hazards that affect old glass. Exposure to centuries of rain and polluted atmosphere, or the fumes from heating systems in churches, can cause the glass to become etched and pitted, as acids leach out some of the alkaline components of the glass. Although not an infallible sign of antiquity, a silvery appearance, produced by the large number of tiny pits on the outside surface of

old glass, is a useful guide to the presence of such glass in a window. This source of damage continues, and, indeed, is accelerating. In 1974, barely twenty years after releading and repair, thought to be good for many more decades, the glass at Canterbury Cathedral was discovered to be in imminent danger through the effect of pollution, which in some places had reduced the thickness of the glass to one third. The only hope for preservation is to 'plate' each piece after cleaning, a long and expensive operation.

2
THE SPONSORS AND MAKERS OF STAINED GLASS WINDOWS

FIGURES of donors are not represented in stained-glass windows until the second half of the fourteenth century, and it is only then that we can begin to identify some of the sponsors of the windows. Undoubtedly, the Church commissioned much of the early work, especially in the wealthy monastic foundations. Canterbury Cathedral derived a considerable income from donations by pilgrims to Thomas à Becket's shrine, and the twelve windows of the Trinity Chapel were filled with panels illustrating the miracles worked there. Such graphic testimonials to the efficacy of St Thomas's powers, like the modern advertisements they resemble, would have brought a considerable return on the original 'investment'. Individual churchmen were often donors. They range from great ecclesiastics like Bishop Skirlaw of Durham, who paid for the great east window at York Minster, and Cardinal Thomas Langley, who donated the St Cuthbert window in the same church, through lesser clerics like Adam de Murimonth, canon of Hereford, who presented the east window of Eaton Bishop, Hereford-shire, to humble priests such as John Eycote, rector and donor of a window in North Cerney church, Gloucestershire. However, much of the medieval stained glass was presented by laymen. The records of donations in three churches of different size show the variety of people who sponsored windows.

When the fourteenth-century nave of York Minster was glazed, windows were presented by Thomas de Beneston, keeper of the fabric, Robert de Riplyngham, Chancellor of the Minster, Richard Tunnoc, bellfounder, and the wealthy families of le Dene and de Mauley. In Saint Michael le Belfrey, a large town church in York, the nave windows were glazed around 1530, and paid for by Martin Soza, goldsmith and sometime Sheriff of York, John Listar, master tailor, Sir Christopher Seel, Chanter of the Church of York and clerk of the works, John Coltman, subtreasurer of the Church of York, and John and Robert Ewald, Mayor and Sheriff of York. At the other end of the country, the windows of the remote parish church of St Neot, Cornwall, were sponsored by the local families of Harys, Martyn, Colway and Burlas, with two of the nave windows presented by the women and maidens of the parish, in the early sixteenth century.

Occasionally, all the windows of a church might be glazed as the gift of one man. One of the most notable examples of such generosity is the church of Fairford, Gloucestershire, built and glazed as the gift of John Tame, a woolstapler and cloth merchant, at the end of the fifteenth century. John Clopton, a clothier, rebuilt Long Melford church, Suffolk, around 1480, with new windows throughout. Unfortunately, only a little of the glass he sponsored has survived. Windows were given by trade and religious guilds; the recently restored Corpus Christi procession

Above, right: French panel, perhaps from Le Mans Cathedral, first half of the twelfth century – Twycross Leicestershire; *above, left*: 'Lamech', *c.* 1178 – south-west transept, Canterbury Cathedral; *below*: 'The Presentation of Christ', from St Denis, Paris, mid-twelfth century – Twycross, Leicestershire

window in All Saints, North Street, York, was probably the gift of the Corpus Christi Gild of that city. Some windows were commissioned by Royalty. The large window in the north-west transept of Canterbury Cathedral was ordered in 1465 by King Edward IV, while the 'Magnificat' window in the north transept of Great Malvern Priory was paid for by Henry VII, around 1501. The west window in the same church had been sponsored by Richard, Duke of Gloucester, later King Richard III, around 1480.

The usual motive for presenting windows, as with other gifts to the church, was invocatory. Requests to pray for the soul of the donor are constantly met with in inscriptions in medieval windows. Presentations to monastic churches ensured the continuing prayers of the community for the donor, while a bonus could be expected in the form of intercession in heaven by the saints depicted in the glass. The donor's choice of subject for the windows he presented might be governed by his trade. Each had one or more patron saints who were especially responsible for their wellbeing (see Chapter four). A woman donor might choose to represent a female saint such as St Margaret, who was invoked for assistance during childbirth.

Some windows had the additional function of commemorating particular events; several are 'war memorials'. The Battle of Neville's Cross was commemorated with figures of the four sons of Ralph Neville, Earl of Westmorland, in glass of around 1350 at Well, Yorkshire, while seventeen archers of Sir Edward Stanley's force at Flodden appear in glass of 1524 at Middleton, Lancashire. At Fladbury, Worcestershire, there is heraldic glass, from Evesham Abbey, with the arms of participants in the Battle of Evesham. The most impressive of all the memorial glass is in the huge east window of Gloucester Cathedral, donated around 1350 by Lord Bradeston to commemorate the Battle of Crécy, with the arms of some of the participants surmounted by row upon row of kings, ecclesiastics, saints and angels.

The costs of production of stained glass are known from rolls of account, contracts and so on which survive from the fourteenth to the sixteenth centuries. A detailed account of the glazing of St Stephen's Chapel, Westminster, in 1351 is given in the Westminster Rolls. The total cost of work from 20 June to 28 November was £145. The master glaziers who designed the windows as well as painting some of the glass were paid one shilling a day; other workmen painting the glass to the master's designs received sevenpence a day. Those cutting and joining the glass had sixpence, while the 'glazier's boys' whose job was grinding the colours for the enamel got fourpence-halfpenny. To put these wages in perspective, it must be remembered that a reasonable income for a gentleman or small landowner was from £10 to £20 a year, while a knight with an annual income of £150 was considered rich. In 1389 Chaucer was paid two shillings a day as Clerk of the Works of the Palace of Westminster, the Castle of Berkhamsted and other properties. This salary of around £36 a year must be compared with that of a senior civil servant today to obtain a true picture of real income in medieval times. On this comparison, the glass workers were quite well paid. The Westminster accounts also give some of the costs of materials: iron bars, or sondlets, for supporting the glass panels cost twopence a pound, two hundred closing nails cost eighteenpence. Tin was threepence a pound and grosing irons for trimming the glass were a penny-farthing each. Glass bought for the chapel was around eightpence for five pounds of white glass, while blue glass cost three shillings and sevenpence for five pounds. Red glass was two shillings and twopence for the same quantity.

Above : 'The Virgin and Child' *c.* 1200 – east window of the crypt, Canterbury Cathedral; *below :* 'King Louis VII of France visited by St Thomas in a dream', *c.* 1220 – Trinity Chapel, Canterbury Cathedral

Early in the fifteenth century John Thornton, a Coventry glazier, was asked to paint the east window of York Minster. His contract, agreed in 1405, called for the work to be completed within three years, for which he would receive four shillings a week, with £5 at the end of each year. If the work was carried out to the sponsor's satisfaction he would receive a bonus of £10. His total payment for three years' work, provided with materials and labour by the Dean and Chapter, would have been around £56. For this he designed and painted a window seventy-two feet high and thirty-one feet across. The most interesting account of a commission for stained glass is found in the contract for the windows of the Beauchamp chapel at Saint Mary's church, Warwick. It was between the executors of the late Richard Beauchamp, Earl of Warwick, and John Prudde, glazier, of Westminster. The contract is worth quoting at length, for the picture it gives us of the relationship between sponsor and craftsman:

> John Prudde of Westminster glasier 23 Junii 25 Hen. 6 covenanteth &c. to glase all the windows in the new chapell in Warwick with Glasse beyond the seas, and with no Glasse of England; and that in the finest wise, with the best, cleanest, and strongest Glasse of beyond the seas that may be had in England, and of the finest colours; of blew, yellow, red, purpure, sanguine, and violet, and of all other colours that shall be most necessary and best to make rich and embellish the matters, images, and stories, that shall be delivered and appoynted by the said executors by patterns in paper, afterwards to be newly traced and pictured by another painter in rich colour, at the charges of the said Glasier. All which proportions the said John Prudde must make perfectly to fine, glase, eneylin it and finely and strongly set it in lead and souder it as well as any Glasse as in England. Of white Glasse, green Glasse, black Glasse, he shall use put in as little as shall be needful for the shewing and setting forth of the matters, images and storyes. And the said Glasier shall take charge of the same Glasse, wrought and to be brought to Warwick and set it up there, in the windows of the said chapell: the executors paying to the said Glasier for every foot of glass, ii shillings and so for the whole xci. li. is. xd.

This price of two shillings a foot for the finest glass is the highest of which there are records; Prudde had lower rates for more ordinary jobs. The lowest rate was eightpence halfpenny a foot for figures of saints, probably from old cartoons, on plain backgrounds; tenpence a foot was charged for heraldic glass with decorated backgrounds, and one shilling a foot for a figure within an ornamental border. Subject windows with much detail would cost from one shilling and twopence to one shilling and fourpence, depending on the work involved.

The glazing of the chapel of King's College, Cambridge, was another expensive project for which records survive. The work was begun by the King's Glazier, Barnard Flower; on his death, contracts were made with other glaziers to complete the work. One contract, signed on 3 May 1526, between the College authorities and the London glaziers Galyon Hone, Richard Bownde, Thomas Reve and James Nycholson required that:

> they schalle at their owne propre costes and charges well, suerly, clenely, workmanly, substantyally, curyously and sufficiently glase and sette up, or cause to be glased and set up eightene wyndowes of the great churche within the Kynge's college of Cambridge, whereof the wyndowe in the este end of the seid churche to be oon, and the wyndowe in the weste ende of the same churche to be another; and so seryately the resydue with good, clene, sure and perfyte glass and oryent colors and imagery of the story of the olde laws and of the newe law after the forme, maner, goodeness,

curyousytie, and clenelynes in every poynt of the glasse wyndowes of the Kynge's newe chapell at Westmynster.

The work had to be finished within four years, and the glaziers were contracted to "suerly bynde all the seid wyndowes with double bands of lead for defence of great wyndes and outrageous weatherings." They were to be paid twopence a foot for the lead required and "for the glasse workmanship and setting up twenty foot of the seid glasse by them to be provided, wrought and sett up after the forme aboveseid eightene pence sterlinges."

The first glass-workers in England appear to have been brought over from France. A treaty between Henry II and Louis VII of France permitted one of the leading French glass-painters to emigrate to England to carry on his craft here. The close relationship between the religious foundations at Canterbury and Chartres clearly led to links between the craftsmen working at the two sites. Certainly there is a very close similarity between the twelfth- and early-thirteenth-century glass at the two Cathedrals, the artists being probably French in both cases. The panel from a Jesse Tree of around 1150, in York Minster, was also French work. The earliest reference by name to an English glass-worker is of Edward, appointed master glazier at Windsor in 1242, although there were many earlier but ambiguous references to individuals called Verarius, which may refer either to glass-making or glazing. The names of more than a dozen glass-workers are known from the first half of the thirteenth century, and the number increases to thirty-two during the second half. At this time they were described as 'verrours' or 'verrers', from the French *verre*, glass. During the following century this title gave way to that of 'glasswryght', from the Anglo-Saxon for worker, and this in turn changed to 'glasier' or 'glayser' around the beginning of the fifteenth century.

The glaziers, like all medieval craftsmen, organised themselves into guilds, which, like the modern trade unions, protected their members by making regulations governing hours of work, conditions of apprenticeship and so on. The larger guilds, like that of the London Glaziers, exerted a considerable pressure against the employment of foreign glass-workers who were not guild members, enjoying some success until King Henry VII and King Henry VIII encouraged the immigration of artists and craftsmen, giving them licences to work without restriction, and commissioning major works from them. A high proportion of the glass produced in this country from the end of the fifteenth century until the Reformation was painted by Flemish or German craftsmen.

The names of many medieval glass-painters are known, but only a few can be identified with surviving glass. One of the earliest glaziers of note was Thomas of Oxford, who painted the late-fourteenth-century glass in the antechapel of New College, Oxford. Some panels of a Jesse Tree from this chapel are now in York Minster. Thomas also designed the glass in Winchester College chapel, and his figure was included in the glass with those of other craftsmen employed on the building. John Thornton, of Coventry, already referred to, must have had, in his time, a high reputation to have been employed on such a major job as the glazing of the east window at York Minster. This extraordinary achievement ranks as one of the masterpieces of the art of stained glass. The tracery has one hundred and seventeen compartments, filled with figures of angels, prophets, patriarchs and saints; in the upper part of the main lights are twenty-seven panels illustrating the Creation and other Old Testament scenes. Below is the remarkable representation of the Apocalypse, based on Revelations, occupying eighty-one panels, and at the bottom of the window are figures of kings and saints, together with heraldic glass. Thornton may also have painted the glass in the north window of Saint Mary's Hall, Coventry, and, perhaps, the 'Pricke of Conscience' window at All Saints, North Street, York.

John Prudde, the King's Glazier, was another talented glass-painter. His post went back at least to the first half of the thirteenth century; in 1290 John of Bristol held the position, and Roger Gloucester was appointed in 1412. John Prudde replaced him in 1440 to hold for life

> the office of glasyer of the King's works, to hold in such fees and wages as Roger Gloucester held, by the hands of the clerk of the works, and all other appurtenants, profits and a 'shedde' called the 'glasyer's logge' in the western part within Westminster Palace, and a gown of the King's livery of the suit of the sergeant of the works yearly at Christmas.

Prudde's major achievement was the glass in the Beauchamp chapel, at Warwick, St Mary, the contract for which was quoted above. The remaining glass, although badly damaged, is the finest and richest of its period to be seen in England. Prudde clearly gave his sponsors their money's worth in the intricate designs and brilliant coloured glass. Other surviving work by Prudde is at Margaretting, Essex, in a Jesse Tree in the east window. He may have painted glass at Bledington, Gloucestershire, and the figures of kings in the west window at Canterbury Cathedral. Little or nothing survives of the glass he is known to have made for Fromond's Chantry at Winchester College, and the Hall and Chapel of Eton College.

William Neve received the appointment of King's Glazier in 1476. He was responsible for the 'Royal' window in the north-west transept of Canterbury Cathedral, commissioned by Edward IV and displaying richly coloured figures of the King and his family against backgrounds patterned with badges. He may have been responsible also for the very similar figures of kings in St Mary's Hall, Coventry, and for glass in the chapel of Christ's College, Cambridge. The German Barnard Flower was another King's Glazier, holding the post from 1505 until his death in 1517. He worked on the glass for Henry VII's Chapel, Westminster, and on four windows of King's College Chapel, Cambridge. He may well have been responsible for the windows of Fairford church, Gloucestershire.

The practice of glass-painting in England probably began in centres such as Canterbury and York, where much building was in progress, with enough business to support a group or 'school' of craftsmen. As demand grew, manufacturing centres sprang up all over the country, usually within easy reach of the ports through which the raw materials were imported. There were major centres at Westminster, Oxford, Gloucester, Winchester, Norwich and York, and there were glaziers working in Bath, Canterbury, Chester, Chichester, Colchester, Coventry, King's Lynn, Lewes, Lincoln, Southwold and Wells, and, doubtless, many other places, including villages as small as Lenton in Nottinghamshire, which is known to have had a glass-painting family in the middle of the fourteenth century.

There are similarities of style and detail which enable work in widely separated churches to be attributed to the same 'school' of glass-painters. These similarities may be due to the creative influence of one man, or the re-use of a stock of cartoons. In Cley church, Norfolk, is a fifteenth-century figure of St Agatha, which is so similar to one at St Peter Hungate, Norwich, that they must have been painted from the same cartoon. The churches at Fladbury and Warndon, Worcestershire,

St Agatha, drawn from the same cartoon, fifteenth century, Norwich school; *left :* St Peter Hungate, Norwich; *right :* Cley, Norfolk

both have similar panels of the Virgin and Child, of the fourteenth century. They are quite unlike any other representations of this subject elsewhere in England. Close similarities of fourteenth-century glass at Eaton Bishop and Brinsop, in Herefordshire, and Mamble, in Worcestershire, notably in the use of a coloured glass trellis pattern as a background to figures, suggest they have a single source. A similar design at Bere Ferrers in Devon may have been by the same firm. Representations of Christ in glass at Crudwell, Wiltshire, Sherborne Abbey and Melbury Bubb, Dorset, and East Brent, Somerset, all have similar characteristics, notably in the drawing of the head. The face tapers down to a narrow chin, with a small forked beard, a feature also seen in a figure of St Edmund in North Cadbury church, Somerset. All probably have a common origin.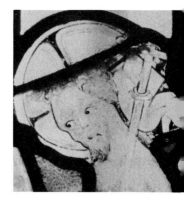

Some techniques appear to have a regional distribution. One, more common in the west country than elsewhere, is the fifteenth-century practice of leading-in ornament. A small piece of coloured glass is set with leads in a hole cut in a larger piece, to give the effect of jewelled ornament. This rather difficult and intricate technique was used for glass surviving in a number of churches in the west, among them St Weonard, Cornwall, Great Malvern Priory, Worcestershire, Gloucester Cathedral, Stanton, Buckland and Fairford, Gloucestershire, and Ludlow, Shropshire. Other examples can be found as far away as Clavering, Essex, Denston, Suffolk, and Warwick, St Mary. At St Michael, Spurriergate, York, an alternative method of embellishment was used. Small pieces of coloured glass were cemented on white using a soft glass flux as an adhesive. It was employed to add 'jewels' to the edge of a *mandorla* or radiance surrounding figures of the Trinity. This technique was mentioned in Theophilus's work, but does not appear to have survived in many places.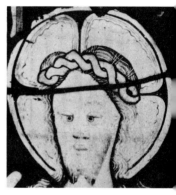

In the fifteenth century there were three centres of glass-painting that developed distinctive styles, whose work was not confined to a limited area and of whose glass sufficient survives to be identified and assessed. These centres were at Norwich, York and in Somerset. The history of glass-painting in Norwich goes back at least to the end of the thirteenth century, when Nicholas Fayerchild was working on windows in Norwich Cathedral, but it flourished in the fifteenth century. At that time a wave of building new churches and rebuilding old ones, financed by merchants grown rich in the wool trade, gave much business to the glaziers. The names of almost thirty glass-workers in Norwich are known from this period, and there were sure to have been others. The Norwich work is inventive, well drawn and vigorous in style, and the glass-painters developed several motifs which were used with such regularity as almost to constitute trademarks. The most recognisable of these is a pattern used to simulate knotting and graining of wood, having the appearance of rows of ears of barley. It can be seen in the glass of many East Anglian churches. Glass clearly painted by several artists incorporates the device, and it has been suggested that it was introduced by one firm around the middle of the century and gradually taken up by others, until by the end of the century it was in general use. Other characteristics of the Norwich glass include borders of spiky, holly-like leaves wreathed around vertical rods, distinctly different from the leaf and rod pattern elsewhere, and an attenuated version of the 'seaweed' pattern backgrounds popular in the fifteenth century.

The oldest glass *in situ* in England is believed to be a panel from a Jesse Tree of around 1150, in a north nave window of York Minster. This panel is so like others at Chartres and St Denis in France that it was probably made abroad, or by a visiting glazier from France. It is probable, however, that early on a group of glass-painters were in business in York, whose Cathedral and many parish churches, together with those of the surrounding towns and villages, would have provided them with ample custom. Between 1313 and 1540 as many as a hundred glaziers were listed among the freemen of York. A feature which distinguishes York glass of the fourteenth and fifteenth centuries is the presence of small figures in the side shafts and pinnacles of canopies. There are figures shown in this way in the Peter le Dene window in the nave of York Minster, in the fifteenth-century windows of All Saints, North Street, York, and in glass as far away as Newark, Nottinghamshire. Such figures often appear in German and Flemish work, notably in the great monumental brasses at St Margaret's church, King's Lynn,

Opposite : Heads of Christ painted by the same artist or from the same workshop, in the fifteenth century; *top to bottom :* East Brent, Somerset; Sherborne Abbey, Dorset; Melbury Bubb, Dorset; Crudwell, Wiltshire

Glass from the Norwich school of glass-painters, fifteenth century; *left :* The 'ears of barley' motif – Victoria and Albert Museum, London; *above :* The 'holly leaf and rod' border motif

Norfolk, or in the brass to Sir Hugh Hastings at Elsing in the same county. Other evidence of Rhenish influence in York glass can be seen in details of costume and head-dress, very similar to continental work. Since glass for the York glaziers was imported from the Low Countries and the Rhineland through the port of Hull, such influences were to be expected. A peculiar characteristic of York glass in the fifteenth century is seen in the treatment of heads, especially the drawing of the eyes. They are often painted with a wide-eyed look, showing the whole of the pupil, which is normally partly covered by the eyelid. It is quite different from the conventional representation.

There is little evidence of any sizeable group of glass-painters in Somerset before the fifteenth century. The fourteenth-century glass at Wells Cathedral has few similarities with other glass in England. It may have been painted by London glaziers whose work has not survived elsewhere. The heads in the tracery of windows in the Lady Chapel at Wells are rather like others of the same period in the east end of Cologne Cathedral, Germany. There is no indication as to whether there was a single centre for glass-painting in Somerset in the fifteenth century, or whether the firms were scattered over the county. The names of only a few glaziers are found in local records, but there is clear evidence of a firm or group of firms supplying glass in the county and those nearby. The most obvious feature of the work of this 'school' is the distinctive decorative pattern used in the quarries (lozenge-shaped panels) which fill the backgrounds in many windows. It is based upon a fleur-de-lis design, and appears throughout Somerset and neighbouring counties, in many variations. Glass still to be found in a number of west-country churches shows similarities suggesting a common source. The Crucifixion windows at Trull, St Catherine's, Bath and Winscombe, with remains of the same subject at Pitcombe, Doddington and Dinder, all possess common features. The figures of Christ at Crudwell, East Brent and elsewhere, mentioned earlier, may have been Somerset work. They are similar to figures at Langport, Cheddar and Charlinch in Somerset and Kingskerswell in Devon, and it has been suggested that Bristol or Gloucester may have been the source. Glass of Somerset origin is found in Devon, at Doddiscombleigh, for instance, where the windows of the north aisle have the fleur-de-lis motif, and border patterns like those in Somerset churches. In Dorset the windows of Sherborne Abbey and Sherborne Hospital may have been by a glazier from Somerset, or trained in the Somerset style. The fragment of heraldic glass at Sherborne Abbey, showing grosing irons, is possibly connected with a local glazier responsible for this work, as well as that at Thornford, Marnhull, Brympton D'Evercy and Norton sub Hamdon.

3
CHANGING STYLES OF MEDIEVAL GLASS

THE first attempt to distinguish the various characteristics of medieval glass of different periods was written by Charles Winston in 1847. He divided stained-glass making into four periods: Early English, from the earliest glass to 1280; Decorated, from 1280 to 1380; Perpendicular, from 1380 to 1530; and the Cinque Cento, from 1500 to 1550. These periods correspond closely with the changing architectural styles bearing the same names, and of course, the two were closely interdependent. There were long periods of transition, however, since each style took many years to come into general use. For the sake of simplicity and convenience we will consider the periods of glass-painting by their century: Romanesque, of the twelfth century; Early English, of the thirteenth century; Decorated, of the fourteenth century; Perpendicular, of the fifteenth century; and Renaissance, of the sixteenth century. Glass having characteristics of two styles will be found, made during transitional periods, and in addition there was work by glass-painters remote from the major centres who continued in the old style for years after it ceased to be fashionable. These divisions, then, are somewhat imprecise, and should be used only as convenient labels to identify the main types of stained glass.

Romanesque glass of the twelfth century
No English glass survives which can be identified positively as being older than around 1150, although it is possible that a small window of geometrically arranged, largely plain glass at Brabourne, Kent, may be older, perhaps much older. The panel from a Jesse Tree, in a north-west window of the nave of York Minster, is probably from the earlier church of St Thomas of Bayeux, on the same site, pulled down in 1154. It is very similar to panels of the same subject at Chartres Cathedral and the Church of St Denis in Paris, both painted around 1145. It is probably the oldest painted glass made for, and surviving in, an English church. At Twycross, Leicestershire, are a number of panels brought from France. They include a representation of the Presentation of the Infant Christ, from St Denis, which might be contemporary with the Jesse Tree panel. In the same church at Twycross are remains of panels from Le Mans Cathedral, which has glass dating from around 1100. From the style of drawing of at least one of them, it could be from the first half of the twelfth century. Canterbury Cathedral has the greatest amount of Romanesque glass of any English church. The large figures of Patriarchs and Prophets, originally in the choir clerestory windows but now in the west and south-east transept windows, date from around 1178, as do the centre panels of the north-east transept rose window. Two figures from a Jesse Tree, in the Corona

north window, are probably a little later. At Lincoln Cathedral there are figures of kings from a twelfth-century Jesse Tree in the south aisle east window. Apart from imported French glass at Rivenhall, Essex, and Wilton, Wiltshire, and medallions at St Denys, York, there is little other glass in this country dating from before 1200.

As we have already seen, the earliest windows were made by leading together small pieces of rather thick and uneven glass in the manner of a mosaic. The picture windows surviving from this time are almost entirely of coloured glass. Pattern windows of white glass, like that at Brabourne, are uncommon until the following century. A major part of the design was carried by the dark line of the lead, and the painted details were subsidiary. These details, painted in enamel, were simple and stylised. The lines of drapery were stiff and accentuated, following closely the limbs and bodies of the wearers. Faces were drawn with a distinctly Byzantine character, oval with prominent, staring eyes, and almost invariably on brown or deep-pink glass. Bodies were elongated, and hands and feet were often poorly drawn. Where shading was employed, and it was used very sparingly, it was executed in a thin wash of enamel smeared on the glass. Inscriptions, almost always in Latin, were made on white or yellow glass by overpainting with the enamel and then using the stick end of the brush to scrape out the form of the letters, as Theophilus had recommended. This 'light on dark' lettering was called Lombardic, and persisted until around 1375. Details of landscapes or architecture were limited to a few stylised items, and the backgrounds to figures were in plain unpatterned glass, often blue.

The Tree of Jesse must have been one of the most popular early subjects, to judge by the number of surviving examples, although it is less likely to have attracted the attention of the iconoclasts. A literal representation of the family tree of Christ, through the House of David, it was shown as a tree springing from Jesse, the father of David, with figures of his descendants in the branches, and with the Virgin and Child at the top. The earliest examples were simple, confined to one window, and with only a few figures. The foliage of the tree was stylised, in the Romanesque manner, with leaves and branches filling the spaces between figures. The examples at Canterbury Cathedral, in the Corona, and in the nave at York Minster have already been mentioned.

The medallion window was another popular form. The bars across the narrow early windows divided them into square or rectangular compartments. Where the windows were wider, vertical bars were added to make a grid, with the same effect. This regular pattern was followed by the glazier, who produced square panels containing a circular picture or medallion with a decorative border. Patterns of foliage or other motifs were used to fill up the corners. The border to the picture usually had a 'string of pearls' pattern, with thin strips of white glass painted with the enamel to give an effect of a series of small circles touching each other.

Figure windows of this period survive only at Canterbury Cathedral. A series of figures of prophets and patriarchs, seated in a variety of poses, were originally in the choir clerestory windows, but are now in the west and south-west transept windows. There is a simple canopy with a rounded Romanesque arch above most of them. There is also a lively figure of Adam, of around 1190, digging with an iron-shod wooden spade, with a stylised tree in the background, in the west window. At Rivenhall in Essex there are two incomplete figures of bishops, wearing the flattened mitre in fashion in the twelfth century, standing under rounded arches. They were brought in the last century from the church of St Martin at Tours, Chenu-sur-Sarthe, France.

Rose windows are more common in France than in England, where the only one of the twelfth century is in the north-east transept at Canterbury Cathedral. Made around 1178, the centre panels show the 'Old Dispensation', with figures of prophets and the Virtues Prudence, Justice, Temperance and Fortitude. The surrounding panels are nineteenth-century restorations.

Early English glass of the thirteenth century

Towards the end of the twelfth century the influence of the new 'Gothic' style, which had effectively begun with the building of the church of St Denis in Paris by Abbot Suger, reached England. The rounded Romanesque arches and window heads began to give way to the pointed arch, and the architectural style known as Early English emerged. During the thirteenth century the slim lancet windows began to be grouped together, usually in twos, threes or fives. Rather greater quantities of painted glass survive from this period. Canterbury Cathedral has considerable remains of glass from around 1200 in the choir north windows, and of around 1220 in the east window of the Corona and in a number of windows in the Trinity Chapel. Salisbury and Lincoln Cathedrals, and Beverley Minster, have glass of this period, as do a number of parish churches, including Westwell and Nackington, Kent, Madley, Herefordshire, Rivenhall, Essex, West Horsley, Surrey, Lanchester, Co. Durham, Saxlingham Nethergate, Norfolk, Wilton, Wiltshire, and Twycross in Leicestershire.

The mosaic principle employed in the early glass is also characteristic of this

Opposite : Windows of the Trinity Chapel, Canterbury Cathedral, about 1220, showing the shaped iron framework supporting the glass panels
Below : In the thirteenth century the main features of the design were represented by the lead lines, as can be seen by comparing these interior and exterior views of a medallion of St Edmund at Saxlingham Nethergate, Norfolk

period, although the pieces of glass tend to be slightly larger. As before, the lead lines are vital to the design of the window. The drawing of figures and draperies is less stiff, being looser and more flowing than in the previous century. A lighter, pinker glass was used for flesh colour, and facial details, as well as those of hands and feet, became rather more natural. The Lombardic form of inscription continued throughout the century, as did the use of smear shading. Architectural and landscape backgrounds were a little more detailed than before, although still very stylised. From around 1220 the backgrounds to figures were frequently diapered – painted with regular patterns which helped to subdue the amount of light passing through the glass without muddying the colour, as would have happened if a uniform wash of enamel had been applied. A fleur-de-lis motif was common in diapered glass of French origin; it can be seen in panels from France at Wilton, Wiltshire.

The Jesse Tree continued as a popular theme for a window. It was still confined to a single lancet, as in a window at Westwell, Kent. Here, four figures in a vertical line make up the Tree (the bottom two figures are restorations made up from old glass, the originals having been destroyed in a storm early in the last century). The remains of another early-thirteenth-century Jesse Tree can be seen at Nackington, Kent, and parts of what must once have been a very fine example, of the mid-thirteenth century, are in a south nave window of Salisbury Cathedral.

The medallion window continued through this period, and some of the finest examples are at Canterbury Cathedral. At the end of the twelfth century it became the practice in large windows to bend the glazing bars to conform to the outline of the medallions, avoiding heavy shadows which might fall across the pictures and strengthening the overall pattern of the window. The only surviving examples of the use of these shaped armatures are in Canterbury Cathedral, where they are especially obvious where the coloured glass is missing. As in the earlier period, the circular, square or semicircular medallions were edged with borders, often 'pearled', and usually with inscriptions. In the angles and spaces between medallions, stylised foliage patterns were used. These windows normally had wide decorative borders surrounding the groups of medallions. The subjects of the medallion windows now included scenes of the lives and miracles of saints, as well as biblical subjects, usually based upon the type – antitype scheme (see Chapter 4). Canterbury Cathedral has excellent examples of both types, the latter in the north choir aisle windows, and the former represented by the windows of around 1200 in the north choir triforium, showing the martyrdom of St Alphege and the life of St Dunstan. In the crypt chapel of St Mary Magdalene is glass showing the life of St Nicholas, but most impressive of all is the series of large windows, dating from around 1220, showing the miracles worked at the tomb and shrine of St Thomas à Becket. Medallion windows are found elsewhere; at West Horsley, Surrey, there is a panel of the martyrdom of St Catherine, and another of St Mary Magdalene anointing Christ's feet, both of around 1220. The stoning of St Stephen is represented in a mid-thirteenth-century window at Grately, Hampshire. Medallion windows with biblical scenes can be found at Madley, Herefordshire, Wilton, Wiltshire, Twycross, Leicestershire, and Rivenhall, Essex; in the last three churches the glass has been brought from France in recent times.

Figure windows continued in the simple form of the previous century; there are typical examples in the north and south aisle windows at Lincoln Cathedral. Where canopies are present, the arches are pointed, as they are in the panel of a king and bishop in a south nave window of Salisbury Cathedral. Towards the end of the century, figures of saints are shown bearing emblems by which they may be

[29]

recognised (see Chapter 4). At Saxlingham Nethergate, Norfolk, for example, there is a figure of St Edmund, carrying the arrows by which he was martyred. Only a few Crucifixion windows survive from this period; the figure of Christ hangs stiffly on the Cross, with his arms straight along the cross-piece, an unnatural pose. There is a late thirteenth-century example at Wick Rissington, Gloucestershire.

The only rose window from this period is in the north transept of Lincoln Cathedral. Of early-thirteenth-century date, it originally represented a 'Doom', or general resurrection of the dead at the Last Judgement, but many missing panels have been replaced by other, but contemporary, subjects. The south transept rose window in the same cathedral is glazed with fragments only of thirteenth-century glass.

The most important innovation of the thirteenth century was that of grisaille glass (from the French *gris*, grey). It has been suggested that this elaboration of plain glazing was the result of an edict in 1134 by the Cistercian order, discouraging the excessive decoration of churches. But the technique was used in many places where the Order's influence cannot have been strong, and it is more likely that it was the combination of the high cost and light-excluding properties of the coloured mosaic glass that led to the development of a cheaper and lighter glazing scheme around the middle of the century. A grisaille window was made by laying out a regular or geometric pattern in white glass. Upon each piece a stylised foliage motif was painted in enamel, emphasised by crosshatching the background. At first these foliage motifs were confined within each piece of glass, but toward the end of the century the stylised leaves and branches tended to run across the pattern of leadlines, and the crosshatching was discarded. Strips or bosses of coloured glass might be used sparingly to accentuate the pattern, as in the north and south aisle west windows at Salisbury Cathedral. The most remarkable thirteenth-century grisaille windows are the 'Five Sisters' in the north transept of York Minster, but other examples can be seen in the north transept of Lincoln Cathedral, in the chapels of Saint Gabriel and Saint Mary Magdalene at Exeter Cathedral, and at Hereford Cathedral. Figure panels set in alternate rows with grisaille are a development of the later thirteenth century, as represented at Chetwode, Buckinghamshire.

Grisaille and quarry glass; *above, left :* Thirteenth century – Stodmarsh, Kent; *above, centre :* Late-thirteenth century – Exeter Cathedral; *above, right :* Early-fourteenth century – Haslingfield,

Heraldic glass appears in the last quarter of the century. The oldest is in the west window of Salisbury Cathedral, dating from around 1270. The Royal arms in the glass at Chetwode are of about the same date. Shields are set in the grisaille glass of slightly later date at Exeter. The early shields are 'heater' shaped – like the base of the old-fashioned flat-iron, the sides of the shield curved in continuously from the top to a point on the bottom, giving it a roughly triangular shape.

There is foreign glass of this period in several places. Glass from the Randolph Hearst Collection, now in the south choir aisle windows of Canterbury Cathedral, came from France. Rivenhall, Essex, has four beautiful French medallions of around 1200 and a figure of a knight of the same period. At Twycross, in Leicestershire, there are a number of French panels, several of which, of around 1243, came from St Chapelle, Paris. Glass from the same place is at Wilton, Wiltshire, together with many other panels of the thirteenth century. The Victoria and Albert Museum, London, has a French Jesse Tree of around 1250, and the Burrell Collection in Glasgow Art Gallery has other French glass of the early thirteenth century.

Decorated glass of the fourteenth century

The grouping of several lancet windows in the later thirteenth century was sometimes accompanied by piercing of the spaces between the points of the heads of the windows. From this naturally evolved the single large window, divided by vertical masonry, or mullions, into vertical compartments, or lights. The head of the window was filled with decorative apertures, producing tracery. Thus appeared the Decorated style of architecture, in its earliest form around 1280. The shapes of the tracery compartments were at first simple and regular with lozenge-shaped or three-, four- or five-lobed apertures in the geometrical style, but later developed into curved forms, with flowing lines, using the double curve of the ogee, appearing around 1300. These architectural changes were accompanied by significant developments in the glass designed for the new windows.

Considerable amounts of fourteenth-century glass survive throughout the country. There are major quantities at York Minster and Wells Cathedral, for example. Important amounts are at Tewkesbury Abbey and Exeter Cathedral, and many parish churches have examples ranging from whole windows like that at Checkley, Staffordshire, to single but delightful figures like the Virgin and Child panel at Fladbury, Worcestershire. The earliest Decorated glass still retained some of the characteristics of that of the previous period. The medallion form persisted for a short time into the fourteenth century, as at Checkley, where figures of around 1300 are surrounded by the 'string of pearls' beaded borders, or at Newark, Nottinghamshire, where the same technique is used to decorate simple canopies over biblical subjects. The lead line began to play a less fundamental part in the design, especially after the introduction of silver staining. As already mentioned, this new technique was introduced around 1306, the earliest known example to survive being in the Peter le Dene window of around 1308, in the nave of York Minster. The Newark glass, of around 1310, shows some small use of the technique. The ability to portray different parts of the design in yellow on white eliminated some of the previously necessary leadlines, between a crown and the wearer's head, for example.

An important feature of the Decorated glass was the tendency to give figures a less stiff, slightly swayed pose, which in the early fourteenth century developed into a strongly curved pose like a shallow letter S. This persisted throughout the century, although it became less prominent towards the end. The swaying of figures is especially apparent in representations of the Crucifixion, where the figure of Christ hangs down from the cross-piece with His body bent in a double curve. Although pink glass was still used for faces at the beginning of the period, increasingly, white glass began to be used for this purpose. In the east window of Exeter Cathedral six figures painted by Walter of Rouen around 1300 have pink faces, while the rest of the figures in the window, painted by Robert Lyon around 1392, all have faces on white glass. Lombardic inscriptions, now often in Norman French, gave way at the end of the century to black-letter inscriptions, painted in black on white glass.

Following the trend in architectural decoration, a naturalistic representation of foliage developed. Clearly recognisable leaves of oak, ivy, vine and so on appear in grisaille and other glass. Figures were still somewhat stylised, especially at the beginning of the period, but towards the end of the century there were signs of a more natural rendering of figures, drapery, architectural details and so on. Another significant change occurred in the elaboration of the canopy, which had hitherto been more of a symbol than an accurate representation of an architectural structure. In the early-fourteenth-century glass the canopy was simple, straight-edged, with simple crockets or leafy mouldings on the upper edge and with simple, curved surfaces on the lower. It soon became more elaborate, with detailed side-shafts supporting an ornate canopy with the ogee or double-curved arch. The upper side of the canopy, which was often in yellow glass, was covered with very leafy crockets, which were a prominent feature of the masonry of the period. The canopies and side shafts were drawn in flat elevation, with no attempt to render the details of mouldings and carvings in perspective, at least not until the end of the period. The canopies were at first not too ornate, with single pinnacles above each side-shaft and a terminal 'finial' or leafy decoration at the top of the canopy. There is an excellent example of around 1320 above the figure of St Catherine, at Deerhurst, Gloucestershire. In the second half of the century the canopies became increasingly extravagant, with several tiers of shafts and proliferation of pinnacles above the central arch. There are examples of mid-thirteenth-century origin at Tewkesbury Abbey and Hereford Cathedral. The details of the canopies, notably the representations of windows in the side-shafts, show the tracery forms of the period when the glass was painted – geometrical or flowing.

Above: 'Virgin and Child',
French medallion, *c.* 1200
Rivenhall, Essex; *below:*
'Adoration of the Magi',
thirteenth century – Madle
Herefordshire

iapering and background
tterns; *above, left :* Fleur
: lis diaper, French,
irteenth century – Wilton,
iltshire; *above, centre :*
nning foliage diaper,
urteenth century –
orpeth, Northumberland;
ove, right : naturalistic
iage diaper, fourteenth
ntury – Mere, Somerset;
aption continued over)

The space between the edge of the picture and the window masonry was usually occupied by a decorative border, which often included heraldic devices, badges or monograms. Diapering was still used in figure backgrounds, often in the form of a running foliage pattern scraped from a wash of enamel, as in the tracery of the east window at Morpeth, Northumberland, and in several windows at Wells Cathedral. Towards the end of the century a 'seaweed' pattern, a serrated ribbon-like foliage motif, on a larger scale than before, began to replace the diapering.

The glass used in this period was appreciably thinner and lighter in colour than previously, and green and yellow glass (potmetal or silver stained) were used a great deal. A notable example of this can be seen in the east window at Wells Cathedral, where these two colours predominate. In the second half of the century much more white glass was used. This may have been due to a shortage of good coloured glass, as a result of the Black Death which killed many skilled workers in the glass and other trades in 1348 and 1349. Smear shading continued in use, but by around 1380 stippling had been introduced. A smear of pigment was applied to the glass and worked on while still wet with a stiff-bristled brush, which partly removed the enamel and broke the shading up into small dots.

The Jesse Tree maintained its popularity as a glazing scheme, and in the Decorated window the design was spread over the several lights of the larger window. The foliage was now shown in a natural fashion, often as a vine with leaves, tendrils and grapes accurately drawn. The larger window gave scope for many more of the twenty-eight generations of Christ's ancestors to be shown, and to them were often added figures of the prophets who foretold Christ's coming. The recumbent figure of Jesse normally occupies the bottom of the middle lights of the window, with a vine springing from his loins. In loops formed by the vine's branches are the figures of kings and other members of the House of David, and the prophets are shown in panels on either side. At the top of the Tree are the Virgin and Child. The tracery above may contain a 'Doom', as it does in the east window of Wells Cathedral and Selby Abbey; at Morpeth the tracery is filled with scenes of the early life of Christ, and at Shrewsbury St Mary the figures of Apostles accompany the Virgin and a Crucifixion. Another Jesse Tree can be seen in the nave of York Minster, and there are remains of others at Madley, Herefordshire, Mancetter and Merevale, Warwickshire, Lowick, Northamptonshire, Gedney, Lincolnshire, and elsewhere. At Dorchester Abbey, Oxfordshire, there is a remarkable Jesse Tree window in the chancel. The figure of Jesse is carved in stone at the bottom of the window, and the mullions are carved with some figures from the series. Others were portrayed in the glass, although the window is no longer complete. This combination of glass and stone is unique in England.

The making of grisaille glass flourished throughout the fourteenth century, but now the foliage was drawn in a naturalistic style running through the pattern of the window. The intricate and varied shapes of the earlier grisaille glass were replaced early in the century by regular quarries (from the French *carreau*, a small square or lozenge). These small diamond-shaped panes were often painted along two adjacent edges with enamel or silver stain, giving an effect when leaded together of a trellis through which the branches of vine, ivy, oak or bramble trail. There are good examples at Acaster Malbis and Thornhill, Yorkshire, Dunston, Norfolk, and Credenhill, Herefordshire. In many of these places the quarries are used to fill the backgrounds to figures. In several churches in the west country an elaborate version of this scheme employed strips of coloured glass to form a lattice, filled in with quarries of other colours, painted with leaf patterns. Examples of this technique (which is not, strictly speaking, that of grisaille glass) are at Bere Ferrers, Devon, Brinsop and Eaton Bishop, Herefordshire, and Mamble, Worcestershire. The arrangement of alternating rows of grisaille glass and figures or panels, introduced at the end of the thirteenth century, continued well into the fourteenth. There are examples at Checkley, Staffordshire, Hereford Cathedral and at Selling, Kent, all around 1300. Often, where there were large areas of grisaille, small roundels with grotesque figures, lion's heads and so on were introduced, as at Haslingfield, Cambridgeshire. At Dewsbury, Yorkshire, grotesques, dragons and so on are surrounded by quarries decorated with birds and shells. This type of quarry, with a self-contained motif, had largely replaced pattern grisaille by the latter part of the fourteenth century.

In the fourteenth century figure windows became very popular. The figures were arranged in rows across the window, with their canopies making a band of

(*Caption continued from previous page*)
Below, left: Diapering on a shield of Despencer, early-fifteenth century – Fladbury, Worcestershire; *below, centre*: 'seaweed' pattern, fifteenth century – Newark, Nottinghamshire; *below, right*: 'seaweed' pattern, Norwich school, fifteenth century – Framingham Earl, Norfolk

he Crucifixion; *left :* later-
irteenth century – Wick
ssington, Gloucestershire;
atre : later-fourteenth
ntury – Thornhill,
orkshire; *right :* fifteenth
ntury – Woolley,
orkshire

contrasting colour when seen from a distance. An early example of a Decorated figure window is at North Moreton, Berkshire. A later example, of around 1344, is the glass of the clerestory windows of Tewkesbury Abbey, and Wells Cathedral has figure windows of the same period. Saints are almost invariably shown with their emblems. Narrative windows illustrating the lives and martyrdoms of saints become more common during this period. The glass at North Moreton illustrates scenes from the lives of Christ, the Virgin, and Sts Nicholas, Paul and Peter. The life and Passion of Christ are shown in scenes under canopies in a series of panels at All Saint's, North Street, York, in glass of the first quarter of the century. The trefoils, quatrefoils or cinquefoils of the Decorated window tracery are often occupied with figures of saints, with the surrounding space filled in with diapering, as at Mere, Wiltshire, Morpeth, Northumberland, Wells Cathedral and many other places. Crucifixions also appear in tracery compartments as well as in the main lights, as at Allensmore, Herefordshire. Scenes of the Annunciation or Coronation of the Virgin are common in tracery, often with the two figures of the Virgin and the Archangel Gabriel or Christ in Majesty in adjacent compartments. The smaller apertures in window heads are often filled with angels.

During this period heraldic glass was made in great profusion. The 'heater'-shaped shield persisted, though it tended to become somewhat elongated as time went on. The shields were now often divided vertically into two, combining two sets of arms, a technique known as impaling, or into four, called quartering. Diapering was used to decorate the areas of plain colour on the shields. Heraldic glass was often incorporated into grisaille windows, as at Exeter Cathedral, or placed in window tracery, with angels sometimes bearing the shields later in the

[35]

...NTVR ...CTAS VNTLVMI NH·MEM BRARESECTA

century. Heraldic badges are frequently incorporated in borders. The fourteenth-century glass in the nave of York Minster shows a number of examples of this, for instance in the fourth window from the west on the north side, where the arms of Clare and Mowbray are repeated throughout the border. Other heraldic motifs that appear in many places are the lions of England, the fleur-de-lis of France and the castle of Eleanor of Castile, wife of Edward I.

Around the beginning of the century, figures of donors begin to appear for the first time. They are represented usually as small kneeling figures at the base of the window. They may be in civilian costume, as in the nave window at York Minster mentioned above, where the donor figure carries a model of a window to signify his benefaction. Another donor with a window is shown at St Michael le Belfrey, York, in glass of around 1330. More often, however, the figures are in armour to show their rank, and usually wear surcoats embroidered with heraldic devices. The many examples include Lord Ferrers and his wife, of around 1338, at Bere Ferrers, Devon, a knight of around 1330 at Carlton Scroop, Lincolnshire, and Sir John de Charlton and his sons in the east window of Shrewsbury St Mary, of around 1340. Sometimes the donors are the main subject of the window. The glass presented to Tewkesbury Abbey by Eleanor de Clare around 1344 shows her two husbands and members of the Clare family in armour with heraldic surcoats. Sir Jacob Berners appears in glass of about 1388, in armour, with his crest above him, at West Horsley, Surrey. The most remarkable figures are in the window in the south of the nave of York Minster, commemorating the de Mauley family. Several members of the family are shown, in armour with heraldic surcoats, and the figure of Sir Peter de Mauley in particular is worth examination for the extraordinarily intricate way in which the complex heraldry of his arms has been rendered in glass.

Perpendicular glass of the fifteenth century
The Perpendicular architectural style is distinguished by the way in which the vertical parallel lines of the mullions of the main lights of the windows are continued in the tracery, producing a series of almost rectangular compartments, contrasting with the curved and flowing lines of the previous period. The style began to come into use around 1380, but had made its first appearance in the great west window of Gloucester Cathedral, made around 1350. The stonework of this huge window, seventy-two feet high by thirty-eight feet wide, shows all the characteristics of the Perpendicular style. It is filled with glass which, from a distance, also looks typical of the fifteenth century, using large quantities of white glass, with red and blue the most prominent colours. This combination may have been forced upon the glaziers by a shortage of glass brought about by the effects of the Black Death, which must have been raging at the time the window was painted. If the glass is examined closely, however, it will be seen to be completely in the Decorated style, with the S-pose, the ogee arches, flat elevation in the canopy shaft drawing and so on. A distinct style of glass painting influenced by the new architecture did not appear before the closing years of the fourteenth century. The next hundred years was a great time of building, rebuilding and extension of churches and cathedrals. The new style permitted larger and larger windows, and in some Perpendicular churches the impression is of more glass than masonry. These major changes were financed by the growing prosperity of the country and supported by the relative stability of the nation's affairs. The Wars of the Roses had little effect upon the mass of ordinary people, and the artist-craftsman was able to pursue his work without serious interruption. There is more glass of the

fifteenth century than of any other period surviving in churches throughout the country.

Several important technical innovations were made during this period. The technique, referred to in Chapter One, of abrading flashed red glass came into general use around the middle of the century, although there are examples of earlier uses. Toward the end of the period flashed blue glass was also produced and abraded in the same way, particularly for heraldic subjects. The leading of one piece of glass in another to produce the effect of jewelled ornament has already been mentioned; it was adopted around the middle of the century. Another innovation was the use of silver staining on coloured glass, to vary the colour of details. At Warwick St Mary this technique has been used on both blue and green glass to give subtle colour variations. The lead lines became much less important in the design of the window, and painting and staining took over the major rôle. After 1400 stipple shading predominated, although some smear shading was still carried out. Toward the end of the century much more enamel was being used for shading than before, to give an effect less like a line-drawing and more like a painting. The glass was thinner, more even and lighter in colour; much more white glass was used, with red and blue the most popular potmetal colours. The white glass was less green in tint, the red more scarlet and the blue lighter and greyer than before. In tracery panels silver staining often provided the only colour.

These technical developments were accompanied by changes in style. Figures were now drawn straight, with no trace of the S-curve of the previous period. The figure of Christ on the Cross was represented hanging straight down, without the curved, almost crouching, pose of the Decorated glass Crucifixion. More care was taken in the drawing of faces, which are often very sensitively rendered. General anatomical details were also more accurately portrayed. The 'seaweed' pattern, introduced at the end of the previous century as a device for filling the backgrounds to figure windows, was employed throughout the century. The elaborate borders of the earlier periods were rarely used, but a common border motif in fifteenth-century glass employed leaves arranged in a spiral around a vertical rod. Often there was no border at all between the shafts of the canopy and the sides of the window. Canopies were almost universally made in white glass, embellished in silver stain. The details of mouldings on side-shafts and pinnacles were drawn with some attempt at perspective, although not very successfully. Frequently, the canopy had several arches between the side-shafts, with pendant bosses and vaulting, and was usually surmounted by clusters of pinnacles, turrets and spires. In the latter part of the century the canopies were often reduced in size, or even omitted in some figure or narrative windows. Saints were often shown standing on tiled pavements, which were drawn as in a plan view; since the figure is shown, as it were, in elevation, there is a conflict between the two viewpoints. Inscriptions were in black letter, sometimes in English, although Latin was still more usual.

Patterned grisaille glass was no longer made. Instead, quarries were used to fill up spaces around figures. They might carry individual devices of stylised foliage, flowers, birds and animals, suns, monograms or heraldic badges.

Jesse Tree windows were still made, but may have become less popular, since fewer survive from this period. The general arrangement was similar to that of the fourteenth century, with the design occupying a number of lights. The foliage was now more stylised than in the Decorated period. The north aisle east window at Leverington, Cambridgeshire, although much restored, is a typical Jesse Tree of the Perpendicular period. There are sixty-one figures displayed in five main

Canopies in stained glass; *left to right :* Decorated, c. 1350 – Gloucester Cathedral; Perpendicular, c. 1450 – Great Malvern Priory, Worcestershire; Renaissance, c. 1530 – Stambourne, Essex; Renaissance, Flemish, c. 1535 – Disley, Cheshire

lights and twelve tracery compartments. There is another much restored Jesse Tree of 1499 at Thornhill in Yorkshire. The example at Margaretting, Essex, by John Prudde, is unusual in that the figures are in pairs in loops in the vine. At Combs, Suffolk, the ancestors of Christ are shown in a series of tracery compartments, without a vine. There are remains of a similar series at Stody, Norfolk.

Figure windows are most common, and as well as their emblems saints may be shown with scrolls bearing their name in black letter. The backgrounds to the figures were often in glass of a different colour from that used behind the canopies, and the colours may alternate through the window. Alternatively, the figures might be shown on pedestals, with quarry backgrounds. Occasionally, more natural backgrounds were shown, especially in representations of St Christopher. At Ludlow, Shropshire, there are houses and a windmill in a distant landscape behind him, while at All Saints, North Street, York, he is shown under a canopy, but at the same time he wades through a stream full of fishes!

Narrative windows were at the peak of their popularity in the fifteenth century. Often they show the life and Passion of Christ, or the life of the Virgin, in a series of panels. Others illustrate the lives and miracles of saints, or Old Testament stories. Among subjects which feature for the first time in fifteenth-century windows are the devotional series such as the Seven Acts of Mercy or those showing the rites of the Church, like the Seven Sacraments.

In earlier periods, designs had been confined to single lights, with the Jesse Tree being the only general exception. In the fifteenth century it was not unusual for subjects to be extended across two or more lights. The Crucifixion is commonly

Techniques of shading;
above : stipple shading, early-
sixteenth century –
Chelwood, Somerset; *below :*
smear shading on a head of
Moses, Norwich school,
fifteenth century – Norwich
Cathedral

represented with the Cross in the central light, with the grieving figures of the Virgin and Saint John in the lights on either side. Sometimes, as at Fairford, Gloucestershire, additional figures are shown so as to occupy five lights. The west window at Fairford is used for a single theme, the 'Doom' or Last Judgement. The upper lights contain a replica of the original glass, replaced early in the last century, showing Christ in glory, surrounded by the rainbow-coloured heavenly Hosts. Below, in the centre, Saint Michael is shown weighing the souls of the rising dead. The blessed pass to the left of the window where Saint Peter waits at the gates of paradise, while the damned are carried to Satan on the right of the window, to suffer in the deep red flames of hell.

The tracery lights of the Perpendicular window were normally filled with saints and angels, the latter often playing musical instruments. For the most part, the tracery glass is white with silver stain only, although some coloured glass is used here and there. Since even a small Perpendicular window had a dozen or more tracery compartments, sets of the Twelve Apostles were sometimes displayed in them, as they are at Westham, Sussex.

Heraldic glass continued to be popular during this period. The shape of the shield changed somewhat, the sides being parallel for a short distance before tapering to a more rounded tip than in the earlier glass. By the end of the century the sides of the shield were parallel for almost their entire length, and the bottom was flattened, to give a much squarer shape. The heraldic charges had become more elaborate, and shields were often repeatedly quartered into eight or sixteen parts. Much of the heraldic glass was displayed in the tracery, often held by angels or, later in the century, hung by straps from stylised trees. Merchant's marks, a form of 'tradesmen's heraldry', are shown in some windows, evidence of donations by rich wool merchants, vintners and others. During this period the Royal Arms appeared in a new form. About 1408 the French arms changed from a blue field scattered with fleurs-de-lis in gold to blue with three gold lilies only. This 'France Modern' replaced the 'France Ancient' in the English Royal arms almost at once. Heraldic costume is often shown. Men were represented with tabards over their armour, at first sleeveless, but by the end of the century with short but very wide sleeves. Women were shown wearing mantles embroidered with heraldic displays.

In the fifteenth-century window donors were often shown accompanied by their families, with rows of children behind the kneeling figures of the man and his wife. Sometimes, as in the contemporary monumental brasses, a man would be shown with two or even more wives, each with the children of the marriage, a reminder that women often died young, in childbirth, and many men remarried, some several times. At Canterbury Cathedral, Great Malvern Priory and Little Malvern there are representations of Royal benefactors, kneeling at prayer desks. It is very unlikely that these, or those of more humble donors, were portraits or even approximate likenesses. They are likely to be conventionalised representations only.

Renaissance glass of the sixteenth century

Royal encouragement of foreign glass-painters at the end of the fifteenth century accelerated the adoption of some of the profound changes in art occurring in the Renaissance, which had begun in Italy around 1420. The new movement emphasised the forms and styles of classical Roman art and architecture, and spread throughout Western Europe in the later fifteenth century. From 1500 much of the glass painted for English churches was made by Dutch or German glaziers familiar with the new style, and they in turn influenced the native glaziers.

Shields in heraldic glass;
above, left to right : Arms of
Eleanor of Castille, *c.* 1300 –
Selling, Kent; *c.* 1500 –
Fifield, Oxfordshire; arms of
Shelton, *c.* 1530 – Shelton,
Norfolk; *below, left to right :*
Arms of de Montfort, *c.* 1400
– Fladbury, Worcestershire;
c. 1530 – St Winnow,
Cornwall; arms of
Macwilliam, *c.* 1530 –
Stambourne, Norfolk

...e drawing of floor tiles;
... : The 'plan view', typical
...he fifteenth century –
...ng Melford, Suffolk;
...*ht* : With 'vanishing point'
...spective, *c.* 1510, Flemish
...hrewsbury St Mary,
...ropshire

The trend towards larger pieces of glass which had continued throughout the Middle Ages reached its extreme at this time. The large panes of glass were treated as surfaces for painting, and the lead line was an undesirable intrusion, to be avoided wherever possible. Enamel and silver stain were used to paint larger areas of glass, and coloured pieces were inserted only where absolutely necessary. Much more paint was applied than ever before, and although this gave great depth and modelling to faces and so on when seen close-to, there was a loss of the brilliance so characteristic of the earlier windows. Perspective drawing, often exaggerated, was used in architectural settings. Floor tiles were drawn in 'vanishing point' perspective. Distant landscapes, often painted on pale-blue glass, could be seen through doorways and windows, giving a great effect of depth. Practically no use was made of patterning in backgrounds, which were generally detailed interiors or exteriors. Black letter inscriptions were often in English. Canopies were reduced to simple arches, of the flattened shape common in Tudor architecture, or rounded in the classical fashion. In glass of continental origin or influence, the canopies were heavily stained in orange silver stain, and showed neoclassical Roman features – rounded arches, with much ornament, spiral decoration on pillars and putti-naked 'cupids'. Abraded red and blue glass, often combined with silver stain, was extensively used, especially for heraldic glass. Painting with coloured enamels, referred to earlier, came into general use around the middle of the century. It had been used first to supplement traditional techniques; examples can be found in the windows of King's College Chapel, Cambridge, painted between 1515 and 1531, and in the Flemish glass now in the Lady Chapel at Lichfield Cathedral, painted around 1535. Panels painted wholly or in great part in coloured enamels, and all of foreign making, can be seen at Southend-on-Sea, Essex, and Thurton, Norfolk, where a panel of the Good Samaritan has white patches where the enamel colours have flaked off, one of the failings of this process.

The Jesse Tree window continued as a source for window design. The sixteenth-century versions have a more detailed design and realistic drawing of the figures. In some examples, the figures are half-length, supported by flowers or leaf clusters. There are several examples in North Wales, including a fine window at Llanrhaidr, Denbighshire, of 1535. There is another Tree at Dyserth in Flintshire, and at Gresford, Denbighshire, the tracery of a window of 1500 in the chancel contains another example. At Southend-on-Sea there is an interesting Flemish panel of around 1525, in which Jesse is shown seated on a canopied throne, with figures of kings suspended around him on stylised branches.

The figure windows typical of the fifteenth century were still produced in the sixteenth, but they tend to be rather overpainted and lack the freshness of the earlier glass. There are a number of such figures, painted around 1530, in St Michael le Belfrey, York. One, of St Christopher, is from the same cartoon used a hundred years before for a window in All Saints, North Street, in the same city. It makes an instructive comparison. Windows at St Neot, Cornwall, painted about 1530, probably by a local glazier, show little of the new fashions, except in a somewhat unsuccessful attempt to convey perspective in the floor tiles. The continental figure windows generally showed detailed interior settings, usually with the donor accompanying the saint, and given almost equal prominence. Examples can be seen at Shrewsbury St Mary; Lichfield Cathedral; Disley, Cheshire; and elsewhere.

Lives of the saints continued to be illustrated in narrative windows. There is a life of St Neot, at St Neot, Cornwall, the miracles of St Bernard of Clairvaux at Shrewsbury St Mary, and the miracles of St Nicholas at Hillesden, Buckinghamshire. The tendency, apparent in the previous century, for a picture to spread over several lights continued in this period. There are examples at Lichfield Cathedral and King's College Chapel, Cambridge. At Great Malvern Priory, the 'Magnificat' window of about 1501 includes a Coronation of the Virgin subject which is spread over three of the six lights, although this gives the window a rather unsatisfactory asymmetrical appearance.

Heraldry features prominently in the sixteenth-century glass. The 'heater'-shaped shield was replaced by more elaborate notched or curved designs, sometimes with scrolled edges. The shields were often surmounted with crests and mantling, a form of drapery, and were often included in panels with donor figures, as at Shelton, Norfolk. Shields continue in tracery compartments, hung from trees, as at Stambourne, Essex. At this church there are good figures of the MacWilliam family in heraldic costume, with effective use made of the abrading technique. Tudor badges, the portcullis, the combined red and white rose and so on, appear frequently in window heads and tracery compartments.

Halfway through the century, the development of stained-glass making in England came to an abrupt halt with the Reformation. Although domestic glazing gave employment to some workers, there was no longer the huge market for elaborate painted glass, and the old skills were soon lost. It was not until three hundred years later that a significant revival of the art took place – but that is another story.

4
RELIGIOUS IMAGERY

For the sponsor of a stained-glass window, its principal function was invocatory, if we discount the obvious functional necessity of keeping out the weather while letting in light, a job done equally well by plain glass. By making as generous a donation as possible, the benefactor hoped for intercession on his behalf in heaven, by the saints he caused to be depicted, as well as expecting the prayers of churchgoers responding to the inscribed requests in the windows. It therefore follows that the content of most medieval glass is directly religious. Heraldry, which will be discussed in the next chapter, is perhaps the only subject that is mainly secular, and even this may have had as its main function the recognition of the important individual or family by the illiterate congregation, from whom prayers were requested. Although the main motive for the insertion of stained-glass windows may have been that of invocation, once installed, no doubt some use was made of them for instruction. Narrative windows based on biblical stories would have provided the parson with useful visual aids in the instruction of the young and illiterate. Windows portraying the duties of a Christian, such as the Acts of Mercy, or illustrating the Seven Deadly Sins would have served as constant reminders to the parishioners, and the fearful scene of the Last Judgement showed graphically what would happen if the right path was not followed. It must be remembered that the majority of the population could not read, and the many visual symbols used in medieval art were not mere abstractions for decorative purposes but vital clues to the layman of the meaning of the window.

Saints and their emblems
The most common form of medieval window shows figures of saints, under canopies or on pedestals, carrying a strange variety of objects, which, to the uninitiated, appear to have no obvious connection with religion. These are the emblems by which the medieval churchgoer, instructed in the lives of the saints, was able to recognise the figures depicted. Such recognition was important, so that prayers could be directed to specific saints, each of whom, it was believed, had a special responsibility for certain groups of people or for certain situations or crises. If a saint was appealed to directly, he or she could be expected to intercede on behalf of the supplicant. St Ambrose wrote:

> They can ask pardon for our sins, since they washed away their own sins, if they had any, in their blood. They are God's martyrs, our advocates, the witnesses of our lives and deeds. We must not be ashamed to beg them to intercede for our weakness, since they knew the weakness of mortal flesh, though they overcame it.

The lives of the saints on which the medieval glass-painter based his images had been set down by many authors, but none was more influential than Jacobus de

Eight popular female saints; *in order :* St Catherine – Mells, Somerset; St Margaret – Martham, Norfolk; St Mary Magdalen – Morley, Derbyshire; St Barbara – Bawburgh, Norfolk; St Dorothy – Middlezoy, Somerset; St Apollonia – North Cadbury, Somerset; St Sitha – Emneth, Norfolk; St Cecilia – Charlinch, Somerset *Colour, overleaf :* 'Christ in Majesty' with Evangelist's symbols and grisaille, mid-thirteenth century – Lady Chapel, Hereford Cathedral

Voragine, an archbishop of Genoa. About 1275 he wrote *The Golden Legend*, a detailed account of the lives of the more important saints. It had been translated from Latin into French by the beginning of the fourteenth century, and Caxton produced an English translation in 1483, adding some stories from the Bible and the lives of some local saints. These stories were a mixture of a small element of fact with a considerable proportion of legend. Most of the early saints had died nearly a thousand years before, and the truth had become overlaid with layers of exaggeration, distortion and misunderstanding. The images of early Christian art had survived where detailed written records had not, and these images were misinterpreted, sometimes with unfortunate results. The story that St Nicholas restored to life three children cut up and pickled by a wicked inkeeper arose through a misinterpretation of earlier representations of the saint with a font containing several diminutive figures, symbols of his prowess as a baptiser. In the legend the font became a pickle tub and the baptised the murdered children. St Erasmus was a patron saint of sailors, and thus was often represented carrying a windlass wound with rope. In later times a legend grew, based on this emblem, that he had been martyred by having his belly slit open and his bowels wound out on a windlass. Images showing saints who, like St Denis, had been martyred by decapitation illustrated them holding their severed heads in their hands, and this gave rise to the story that they had lived and walked after their heads were cut off.

The emblems are usually directly connected with the life or death of the saint, like St Catherine's wheel or St Laurence's grid-iron. Where no such obvious symbol was available, visual puns were sometimes used, like the horn of the Pope St Cornelius (*cornu* = a horn). Some symbols were not specific to one saint: the palm branch signified martyrdom; the book, learning or wisdom; and the sword, death by execution. All the saints were shown with a nimbus, or halo, encircling the head. In the surviving stained glass, which is only a fraction of what was once in our churches, there are represented over a hundred different male saints and approaching half that number of female saints. To give an account of them all here would not be practical; instead we will consider in some detail the most popular saints, based upon the frequency with which they were represented in a sample of over three hundred churches throughout the country. We will begin with the female saints, in order of popularity:

St Catherine of Alexandria was by far the most popular saint, male or female, being represented more times than any other, and images of her account for more than twenty-two per cent of all female saints in the churches investigated. She was the most famous of the 'Virgin Martyrs' who died defending their chastity and faith. She was ordered to be put to death by the tyrant Maximin in 307, by being torn on spiked wheels. The wheels shattered, killing her persecutors, an event shown in a thirteenth-century panel at West Horsley, Surrey. She was finally beheaded. In pictures she always carries the spiked wheel, and usually wears a crown and may hold a sword or a book. She was the patron saint of philosophers, students and spinsters. There is a particularly fine representation of her at Deerhurst, Gloucestershire, and her life is shown in the Peter le Dene window in the nave of York Minster.

St Margaret of Antioch was another popular Virgin Martyr. Her great beauty attracted the prefect Olybrius, who tortured her when he discovered that she was a Christian. While in prison, it was said, she was swallowed by a dragon, which burst asunder when she made the sign of the Cross. After further torture she was

beheaded, in the year 304. Scenes of her life and torture are shown in fifteenth-century glass at Combs, Suffolk. She is always shown trampling on or rising from the belly of a dragon, and carrying a long cross staff. She normally wears a crown. She was the patroness of women, and invoked by them in childbirth.

St Mary Magdalene was one of several women healed by Christ, and who, with Mary the mother of James, was a witness to the fact of the Resurrection. She was believed to be the repentant sinner who washed and anointed Christ's feet, depicted in a thirteenth-century medallion at West Horsley, Surrey, and in the chapel named after her at Canterbury Cathedral. Her emblem is a jar or pot of ointment. She was revered as an acquaintance of Christ, and for her demonstration of the virtues of repentance.

St Barbara was a high-born Syrian of great beauty who attracted so many unwanted suitors that her father kept her locked in a tower. She refused all the royal suitors selected for her by her father, and enraged him by arranging for three windows, symbolising the Trinity, to be fitted in a new building where her father had ordered two. After refusing to sacrifice to idols, she was tortured and killed by her father, who was then struck dead by lightning. The patron saint of artillery-men, she was invoked against lightning, fires and sudden death. She carries a tower as an emblem, and wears the crown of a Virgin Martyr.

St Helena, the mother of Constantine the Great, was converted to Christianity in her old age. In 327 she visited Palestine and founded several churches there. Subsequently, the legend arose that she discovered the True Cross, buried on the site of the Crucifixion. She was also said to have been the daughter of the English King Coel of Colchester, the 'Old King Cole' of the rhyme. The largely legendary story of her life is shown in many panels at Ashton Under Lyne, Lancashire. She is shown crowned and carrying a long cross, or, less often, a shorter T-cross. Like St Barbara, she was invoked against fire and thunder.

St Dorothy, another Virgin Martyr of about AD 300, rejected an offer of marriage from the prefect Fabricus, declaring herself a Christian. She was tortured, but suffered cheerfully, saying she was happy to be entering the Garden of Delights in paradise. After her death by beheading, a basket of heavenly roses and apples was brought by an angel to a sceptical scribe who had mocked her, in fulfilment of a promise made before her death. Thus her emblem is a basket of flowers or fruit, and she usually carries a sword. She was the patroness of gardeners, mid-wives and the newly married.

St Apollonia, said to be an 'aged virgin', suffered tortures during the persecutions of the emperor Decius in the year 250. She had her teeth broken out, and was later burnt to death. She is usually represented as a young woman carrying a tooth in a long pair of pincers. She was invoked against toothache, the unpleasantness of which, in the days before analgesics, must account for her popularity.

St Sitha (or Zita) as a young girl of twelve in 1230 became a servant, remaining one until her death forty-eight years later. She was renowned for her piety and virtue, despite many abuses. Her usual emblems are a bunch of keys, for her calling, and a rosary, for her piety. She was the patron saint of servants, and was invoked for help in finding lost things.

Left : 'Noli me Tangere', th
Risen Christ before Mary
Magdelene, early-fourteent
century – Newark,
Nottinghamshire; *right :*
'Robert Fitzhamon', *c.* 134
choir clerestory, Tewkesbu
Abbey, Gloucestershire

St Cecilia, a member of a third-century Roman family, refused to consummate her marriage with her husband Valerian, who was subsequently converted to Christianity. In some representations she carries or wears a garland of flowers, usually roses, a reference to those said to have been brought from paradise to her and her husband. She is shown in this way at Cley, in Norfolk. After the beginning of the fifteenth century, she is more often shown with a musical instrument, usually an organ; at West Pennard, Somerset, she carries a bell. She was the patron saint of musicians.

St Agatha, a Virgin Martyr of Sicily, was martyred in 251 after refusing the advances of the governor Quintianus. Her breasts were cut off, but were miraculously restored. She is usually represented carrying a severed breast in pincers, as at South Creake, Norfolk, or bare-breasted carrying a flesher's hook, as she is shown at Cley, Norfolk, and St Peter Hungate, Norwich. She was the patroness of wetnurses and bellfounders, and invoked against sterility and diseases of the breast.

Among the other female saints, with their emblems, that may be encountered in medieval glass are St Elizabeth of Hungary (crowned, with loaves or flowers), St Agnes (with a sword and lamb), St Etheldreda (a crowned abbess), St Ursula (crowned, with an arrow and girls hiding in her cloak), St Winifrid (an abbess with a sword and severed head), St Clare (an abbess with the consecrated Host), St Faith (a saw), St Juliana (a chained devil), St Lucy (two eyes on a plate) and St Petronilla (with a key and book).

Male saints can be arranged in two groups – those who normally appear together in sets, such as the Apostles and Evangelists, and the individual saints. We will consider the Apostles first, in the order of their popularity.

St John the Divine was an Apostle and Evangelist, one of the three privileged disciples of Christ. He wrote the fourth Gospel, and, it is believed, the Book of Revelations. Usually shown as a young man, his emblem is a chalice with a winged serpent, a reference to his miracle of rendering harmless a cup of poisoned wine. As an Evangelist, his symbol is an eagle. He was the patron of artists and writers.

St Peter, the second of the inner circle of disciples, in spite of his inconstancy became the founder of the Church at Rome. He was crucified head downwards, at his own request, by the Emperor Nero in AD 64, an event shown in stained glass at North Moreton, Berkshire. Other episodes in his ministry are shown at St Peter Mancroft, Norwich. His emblem is a key, or keys, and he sometimes carries a church and wears a papal tiara. He is often represented with St Paul in figure windows. He was the patron saint of many trades, including fishermen, shipwrights, carpenters and bridge builders, and was invoked against fever, madness, foot trouble and for longevity.

St James the Great was the third of Christ's closest Apostles, beheaded by Herod Agrippa in AD 42. It was said that the ship carrying his body was set adrift and came to rest finally in Spain, where a shrine was built at Compostella. It quickly became a place of pilgrimage, and in the Middle Ages it was the aim of all to make the journey to St James's shrine. Thus his emblems are those of the pilgrim: a staff, purse and a hat with a scallop shell. He was the patron of pilgrims and furriers.

St Andrew was one of the less conspicuous disciples, but became famous through the legends of his missionary work and miracles. He was thought to have been crucified on an X-cross, as shown at Ripon Cathedral in a thirteenth-century medallion, and some of his remains were believed to have been brought to St Andrews in Scotland from Greece. His emblem is the X, or saltire, cross. He was the patron saint of sailors and fishermen, and invoked against gout and stiff necks.

St Bartholemew was martyred by being skinned alive. His emblem is a flaying knife and often he carries his own skin over his arm, as at Grappenhall, Cheshire, and Acaster Malbis, Yorkshire. He was the patron of many trades, most of them concerned with skins, such as tanning, glovemaking, bookbinding and the fur trade.

St Philip was present at the Miracle of the loaves and fishes, when Christ fed the multitude, and thus is usually shown carrying bread, in his hands or in a basket. Alternatively, he may carry a long cross staff. He was the patron of pastrycooks and hatters.

St Matthew was a customs officer who gave up his job to follow Christ. He wrote the first Gospel. He usually carries a sword and a book. As an Evangelist, his symbol is an angel. He was patron of tax collectors.

St James the Less is said to have been related to Christ; he became the head of the Church in Jerusalem. He was believed to have been beaten to death with a fuller's bat (a clothmaking tool) after being thrown from the pinnacle of the temple. His usual emblem is a club, and facially he may be depicted as resembling Christ.

St Thomas Didymus was the disciple famous for his doubts about the Resurrection. Later, he worked as a carpenter in India, where he was martyred by a spear thrust. His emblems are a spear or carpenter's set-square. In legend, he caught the girdle of the Virgin as she was carried to heaven at her Assumption, and he is sometimes shown carrying it, as he is in the east window of Gloucester Cathedral.

St Jude (or Thaddeus) was the brother of St James the Less. He has a variety of emblems, and thus may be confused with other Apostles. Like his brother he may carry a club, but more often holds a boat. He was invoked in moments of crisis.

St Matthias, one of the earliest of Christ's followers, became one of the Twelve following the defection of Judas. Legend has it that he was beheaded with an axe, after miraculous cures at Jerusalem. His emblem is thus an axe or halberd.

St Simon the Zealot was the brother of St Jude, and was martyred with him in Persia. Like Jude, his emblems vary, but most often he carries a saw or a fish.

In trying to identify figures of the Apostles, the reader is warned that many of their emblems appear to have been interchangeable. There is sometimes a conflict between the name on an inscription and the figure suggested by the emblem carried. In addition to the original Twelve, three other Apostles who helped to spread the Word are represented in stained glass:

St Paul, the great Apostle, was a popular figure in medieval art, and is often shown

Five popular male saints, *in order :* St John the Baptist - Almondbury, Yorkshire; St Christopher – All Saints North Street, York; St George – St Winnow, Cornwall; St Lawrence – Pembridge, Herefordshire; St Nicholas – Mere, Wiltshire

associated with St Peter. He was beheaded at Rome by the emperor Nero. His conversion on the road to Damascus and death are shown at North Moreton, Berkshire. He is normally represented as a bald-headed, bearded man with a sword and book. He was the patron of ropemakers, and was invoked against snakebite.

St Luke, the Evangelist and author of the third Gospel, accompanied St Paul to Rome. He was described variously as a doctor or as a painter, whose portraits of Christ and the Virgin converted the heathen. He is usually shown with a book, or, as at Stratton Strawless, Norfolk, with an artist's palette and brush. As an Evangelist, his symbol is a winged ox. He was patron saint of doctors, butchers and painters.

St Mark, the Evangelist and author of the second Gospel, was believed to be the son of St Peter. He went with Paul to Cyprus and Rome, and may have become the first bishop of Alexandria. His emblem is a book, and as an Evangelist, a winged lion. He was the patron of glaziers.

Of the saints other than the Apostles, those occurring most frequently are, in order of popularity:

St John the Baptist, who proclaimed the imminent coming of Christ, appears more often than any other male saint or Apostle. His death at the request of Salome is shown at Gresford, Denbighshire, and in the north transept of York Minster. He is usually represented wearing his hermit's costume of a hairy camel skin, shown with the head still attached, at Holy Trinity, Goodramgate, York. His special emblem is the Agnus Dei, a lamb with a long cross-staff and banner, usually carried on a book. He was the patron saint of tailors and farriers.

St Christopher was an immensely popular saint in the Middle Ages, since it was thought that sight of him each morning would protect one from sudden death during the day. For this reason, a figure of the saint, in glass or wall-painting, was often placed on the north side of the church, opposite the usual entrance, so as to be easily seen on entering, or even, through the door, from outside. In the legend, he was a giant who searched the world for the most powerful king to serve. A hermit told him of Christ, and advised him to settle by a river, where he ferried people across. One day, carrying a child, he felt the whole weight of the world on his shoulders. The infant was revealed as the Christchild and Christopher (his name means Christ bearer) was converted and later martyred. He is always shown with the Child on his shoulder, carrying an uprooted tree as a staff, wading through a stream. He was the patron of travellers, and was invoked for a safe journey.

St George was, by tradition, a soldier of Palestine, who saved the life of a princess by disabling and later killing a dragon, an act which was followed by the conversion of a whole town to Christianity. His life and martyrdom are shown in a window at St Neot, Cornwall, and the episode with the dragon, in a panel at North Tuddenham, Norfolk. As a single figure, he is always shown in the armour of the period when the glass was painted, spearing the dragon with a lance, or striking it with a sword. His shield or surcoat bears a red cross. He was the patron of soldiers and, of course, England.

St Lawrence was a deacon of the Church in Rome, under the Emperor Valerian.

He was martyred in the year 258 by being slowly roasted over a fire, an act illustrated in a French panel at Glasgow Art Gallery. The grid-iron is his emblem, and he is shown wearing the vestments of a deacon. He was the patron saint of cooks, brewers and cutlers, among others.

St Nicholas was a bishop of Myra during the fourth century. His legendary acts include the raising of the pickled children referred to earlier, and the leaving by stealth of three bags of gold as doweries for the daughters of an improverished nobleman. This latter act of charity gave rise to the legend of 'Santa Claus' bringing gifts in secret to children at Christmas. Panels showing his life and miracles are at Hillesden, Buckinghamshire, and North Moreton, Berkshire. He is represented as a bishop carrying three gold balls, or with a tub containing children. He was the patron of young people and pawnbrokers, whose sign is based upon the three golden balls.

St Edward the Confessor was the last Saxon King of England, who founded Westminster Abbey. He is said to have given a ring to an old beggar in Essex, hence the name of the village of Havering; later, pilgrims in Palestine were met by the same old man who told them he was St John the Evangelist, and asked them to return the ring to the King, and to tell him that within six months they would meet in heaven. The story is shown in a window at Ludlow, Shropshire, donated by the pilgrim's or Palmer's Gild. His emblem is a ring, or a church.

St Stephen was the first Christian martyr, stoned to death for his faith. He is shown as a deacon, carrying a cloth filled with stones.

St Edmund was a king of East Anglia, killed by the Danes, who shot him with arrows and then beheaded him. He is shown as a king, holding one or more arrows. He was invoked against the plague.

St Jerome was one of the Four Doctors of the Church, a considerable scholar who translated the Old Testament from Hebrew into Latin. He died in the year 420. He is usually shown with a red cardinal's hat, at a writing desk. Usually a lion is nearby.

St Leonard of Noblac was a French nobleman of the early sixth century, who obtained permission from the king to release prisoners whom he visited. He later entered monastic life and became the first abbot of Noblac. He is shown as an abbot, carrying fetters or chains, and was the patron saint of prisoners.

Among the many other minor saints to be found represented in medieval glass are a group from the British Isles. They include St Cuthbert (a bishop carrying a head), St Dunstan (an abbot with pincers) and St Alphege (an archbishop with an axe). Others without special symbols are the first British martyr, St Alban, St Wulfstan, St William of York, St John of Beverley and St Oswald. The most notable British saint and martyr was, of course, St Thomas of Canterbury. Since his images were systematically destroyed by order of King Henry VIII, few survive, but they can be seen at Canterbury Cathedral, Nackington, Kent, Warwick, St Mary, York Minster, Checkley, Staffordshire, Greystoke, Cumberland, and Lincoln Cathedral.

Other saints, with their emblems, who may be discovered in old glass include: St Anthony (T-staff, bell and pig), St Ambrose (bishop with a beehive) and St

Augustine (doctor's robes), who were, with St Jerome, the Four Doctors of the Church, and are often shown as a group. Other saints are St Martin (dividing his cloak with a sword), St Blaise (with an iron comb or rake), St Giles (abbot with a hind), St Brice (holding live coals), St Denys (bishop holding his severed head), St Vincent (with an iron hook, or cruets), St Clement (Pope with an anchor), St Roch (pilgrim with a plague spot on his thigh), St Sebastian (naked, with an arrow) and St Peter Martyr (with a knife or axe in his head).

The Angels

Angels play a major part in many of the stories of the Old and New Testaments. They were heavenly messengers between God and man, punishing the wrongdoer and protecting the righteous. They constantly praised and worshipped God, rejoicing over the repentance of sinners, bearing souls to heaven, waiting on those in prayer, and when the Last Judgement comes they will help to sort out the blessed and the damned. In the Middle Ages theologians gave much thought to the organisation of the Heavenly Hosts, and concluded that there were Nine Orders of angels, in three hierarchies. The highest orders were the Cherubim, Seraphim and Thrones. They were closest to God, in direct contact with him, and were his counsellors. The Cherubim worshipped him continuously, the Seraphim loved and adored Him and the Thrones supported and sustained His throne. The second hierarchy, receiving glory from the first, were the Dominations, Virtues and Powers, who governed all creation, as the regents of stars and elements, passing glory on to the third hierarchy. These were the Princedoms, Archangels and Angels, who were in authority over mankind. Princedoms governed states and nations, Archangels the cities, and Angels were responsible for individuals.

The Nine Orders were often shown in stained glass, but unfortunately there is no consistent representation, or distinctive emblem, by which each Order can be identified, although often they are named in an inscription. Generally the Cherubim are feathered, with 'eyes' on their bodies and wings, of which there are three pairs. They may carry books, and are often golden in colour. The Seraphim may be coloured red, in part or whole. They may also have six wings, and stand on a wheel (although all Nine Orders are sometimes shown thus). Thrones usually carry scales, representing Divine justice. Dominations may be crowned and robed, but are sometimes shown in academic dress with the beret-like cap of a doctor. Virtues may carry a lamp, and are often shown dressed in white robes. Powers are almost always armoured, with a devil or dragon at their feet. Princedoms are also usually armoured, carrying swords or sceptres. When represented with the other angels, Archangels may have no special emblem, although they may carry sceptres. Angels play musical instruments, swing censers or simply pray. Complete sets of the Nine Orders are found at several places; for example at Sheering, Essex, St Neot, Cornwall, and St Michael Spurriergate, York. There are part sets in a number of places, including four large and striking figures at Great Malvern Priory, Worcestershire.

The Bible names four Archangels who may be represented separately in medieval glass:

St Michael, the Prince of the Heavenly Host, appears in two rôles. He is sometimes shown as an armoured figure with a sword or spear killing a dragon or devil. His wings distinguish him from St George, although he may sometimes also bear the red cross. There are good examples at Trull, Somerset, and Wells Cathedral. In his other capacity he holds the scales of Divine justice, weighing souls against their sins, represented by small devils. He is shown thus at Martham, Norfolk, and in the west window at Fairford, Gloucestershire. He was invoked by those in battle.

St Gabriel is the angel of the Annunciation. He is a kneeling winged figure, carrying a sceptre or a lily, before the Virgin Mary. This scene is represented many times in stained glass. Rarely, he is shown as a separate figure; at Long Melford, Suffolk, he bears a trumpet, perhaps to signify his rôle at the Last Judgement.

St Raphael may be shown in several ways. At Long Melford he is a cloaked, winged figure with a cross chaplet and carrying a sword and book. At Kingsland, Herefordshire, he is with Tobias, who holds a fish, from the story in the Apocrypha. At Bolton Percy, Yorkshire, he applies salve to the eyes of a blind man with a feather – his name means 'medicine of God'. He was the patron of apothecaries, and invoked against eye diseases.

St Uriel is not often represented. There are remains of his figure at Great Malvern Priory, in the 'Magnificat' window, where he carries a book, but the most complete representation is in the fourteenth-century glass at Kingsland, where, as the interpreter of prophesies, he is teaching Esdras.

Ordinary angels are represented in many rôles. They play musical instruments (see Chapter Five), swing censers, carry shields of arms or Passion symbols, attend figures of Christ and the Virgin, especially in Nativity scenes, catch the blood from Christ's wounds, and gently bear the Virgin up to heaven. They almost invariably wear a chaplet with a cross; in the earlier glass they are shown robed, but in the later fourteenth and fifteenth centuries they are covered with feathers. It is assumed that this latter convention was derived from the mystery plays. In these early religious dramas, angels were represented by actors dressed in feathered tights, perhaps to suggest the power of flight possessed by heavenly creatures. The 'eyed' feathers of the Cherubim may have been peacock feathers in the original costumes, to give a specially glorious effect to those representing the angels nearest to God.

Liturgical subjects

The devotional rituals of the church were illustrated in some windows. The *Te Deum* is shown in a simple form at Morley, Derbyshire, where three panels show figures representing the three estates of Holy Church, Martyrs and Apostles. The most remarkable example of an illustration of this liturgical subject is at Gresford, Denbighshire, in the east window donated by Lord Derby in 1500. In the tracery lights is a Jesse Tree, while the upper third of the seven main lights is occupied by large figures. They represent, in the centre, the three figures of the Trinity; to the right are the Archangel Gabriel and the Virgin and to the left are St John the Divine and a figure who may be St Joseph, husband of Mary, since he appears to be carrying a flowering staff. Each figure is surrounded by a mandorla, or radiance, in gold, and the heads of the windows are filled with angels. The bottom two-thirds of the window contains thirty-five panels, each with a phrase from the *Te Deum*. Female saints occupy the outer lights, on each side. On the left are unidentified figures with palms, and on the right the saints carry emblems. The second light from the left shows the Apostles, and the fifth from the left contains male saints with their emblems. Holy Church is represented by monks, popes, archbishops, bishops and other clerics in the third light from the left, and the remaining two lights are filled with the Nine Orders of Angels.

The 'Magnificat' window at Great Malvern Priory illustrates the canticle of 'The Joys of Mary', with verses placed above each panel. Unfortunately, the window has been badly damaged, and much of the design is difficult to understand, but the main arrangement of the window is still apparent. Angels and saints are represented in the tracery lights, while the Coronation of the Virgin is spread over three lights, offset from the middle of the six-light window and surrounded by a mandorla in gold. Panels of the life of Christ surround the Coronation, and large but incomplete figures of the four Archangels occupy the outer lights. The Royal donors appear at the bottom of the window.

The Apostle's Creed was believed to have been composed before they separated for the last time. It is illustrated in the south nave windows at Fairford, Gloucestershire. They show the twelve Apostles, each surmounted by a scroll bearing the appropriate line from the Creed. In windows on the opposite side of the church are figures of twelve prophets, with inscriptions of prophetic statements relating to the Creed. There are remains of Creed windows at other places, including Nettlestead, Kent, and Drayton Beauchamp, Buckinghamshire.

Stories from the Old Testament

The Creation was a popular subject for narrative windows, and the Book of Genesis provided a rich source of images for the medieval glass-painter. There are remains of an early-fourteenth-century series at Newark, Nottinghamshire, where two panels illustrate the creation of animals, birds and fishes, and the expulsion of Adam and Eve from the Garden of Eden. Of fifteenth-century examples, the series at Thaxted, Essex, is incomplete, but those at York Minster, Great Malvern Priory and St Neot are virtually intact. John Thornton's great east window at York Minster illustrates the Creation and the stories of Noah, Abraham, Joseph, Moses, Samson, David and Goliath and the death of Absalom in twenty-seven panels. At Great Malvern Priory thirty-three panels illustrate the story from the Creation to the life of Moses. Two windows at St Neot show the story of the Creation, and the building of the Ark. Sometimes Adam and Eve are shown on their own, perhaps as a reminder to the churchgoer of original sin. Adam digs and Eve spins with a distaff, and both are usually shown naked. Early examples are at Canterbury, of about 1190 (Adam only), Lincoln Cathedral, of the early thirteenth century, and Warham St Mary Magdalene, Norfolk, and Halam, Nottinghamshire, of the fourteenth century. At Martham and Mulbarton, Norfolk, there are fifteenth-century representations, and at Fairford, the Fall is shown, with Adam and Eve eating of the fruit of the Tree of Knowledge. The purpose of these Creation windows may have been simply that of narrative of the origin of the world and the fall of mankind from a state of grace.

Other Old Testament scenes had a more complex purpose. It was a medieval belief that events described in the New Testament were foreshadowed by those in the Old Testament. Great ingenuity was expended in matching the New Testament 'type' with the earlier 'antitype'. In particular two works were important sources of inspiration for the glass-painter: the *Mirror of Man's Salvation* (*Speculum Humanae Salvationis*) and the *Poor Man's Bible* (*Biblia Pauperum*), first produced as manuscripts, but later printed, illustrated by woodblocks. Both were picture-books, the former with one antitype for each type, the latter with two. Probably many churches would have had windows whose content followed this theme; now they survive in a recognisable form at two places only, Canterbury Cathedral and King's College Chapel, Cambridge. At Canterbury there are three windows which follow the type-antitype scheme of the books.

In the north choir aisle two windows, of around 1200, survive of the twelve originally there. They contain panels brought from several other windows, but the upper part of the most westerly one is substantially original, and illustrates the principle clearly. For example, a central medallion showing the adoration of the Magi is flanked on the left by the visit of the Queen of Sheba to King Solomon, and on the right by Joseph's brethren bringing gifts to Joseph. The east window of the Corona, painted some years later, has a more elaborate version of the same scheme. Each New Testament type is surrounded by four antitypes. For instance, the burial of Christ has as its antitypes Joseph cast into the pit, Jonah swallowed by the 'great fish', Daniel in the lions' den and Samson asleep in bed, at the mercy of the Philistines. At King's College Chapel the antitypes are in the upper lights of each window, and the types are below. The Fall of Manna is above the Last Supper and the temptation of Esau by Jacob is the antitype of Christ's temptation in the wilderness and so on. It is probable that a number of isolated panels of Old Testament scenes that survive in various churches were once part of a type-antitype series. An early-thirteenth-century medallion, from France, at Wilton, Wiltshire, shows a figure striking the side of a rock in the shape of a human figure, from whose side water flows. This may well be a symbolic representation of Moses striking a rock in the desert to produce water for the Israelites, the antitype of the piercing of Christ's side, as he hung on the Cross. A series of Flemish panels of about 1500, once at Costessy Hall, Norfolk, are now to be found separated in a number of churches in England, including Exeter Cathedral and Great Bookham, Surrey. One panel has found its way to America. They were clearly part of a type-antitype series. At Exeter, the panels include one of Samson with the gates of Gaza, an antitype for the Resurrection, and a curious subject, Elisha cursing children who had called him 'baldhead' (they were then eaten by bears). Why this subject should be chosen for a church window becomes apparent when we learn that it was given in a Flemish blockbook as an antitype to the mocking of Christ. This subject is featured in a companion panel at Great Bookham. Another panel at Great Bookham shows Joseph being sold to the Midianites by his brothers, the antitype of Judas's betrayal of Christ, which is shown in another panel at Exeter. Also at Exeter, Elisha (or Elijah) is shown restoring the widow's dead son to life by breathing into his mouth. Its companion panel, the scene of Jesus raising Jairus's daughter, is now in the Corning Glass Museum in America.

One of the major Old Testament themes often featured in stained glass has already been mentioned a number of times. The Tree of Jesse, representing the ancestry of Christ back to Jesse, the founder of the House of David, was one of the most popular subjects for the glass-painter throughout medieval times. It is easy to see, when looking at one of the great Jesse Trees, such as that in the east window at Wells Cathedral, why they should have been so, since the glass-painter could exploit to the full the decorative possibilities of a vine with many figures filling a whole window. The religious significance of the design is less obvious. There were in all twenty-eight generations between Jesse and Christ, but usually only the royal ancestors are shown, of whom there were fifteen. In some windows, however, almost all of Jesse's descendants are shown, as in the east window of Selby Abbey, Yorkshire, where they are accompanied by figures of prophets and saints.

The New Testament
As one would expect, a major source of illustrations from the New Testament is the story of the life and Passion of Christ. It seems likely that a great many churches would once have had narrative windows telling this story, but since representations

of Christ were a special target of the iconoclasts in the seventeenth century few have survived. Of these, particularly complete series are at East Harling, Norfolk, St Peter Mancroft, Norwich, East Brent, Somerset, Great Malvern Priory, Worcestershire, St Kew, Cornwall, Elland, Yorkshire, Gresford, Denbighshire, and Fairford, Gloucestershire. Most of these are of the fifteenth century or later; at All Saints, Pavement, York, there is a large series of panels of about 1370 showing scenes of the Passion and events after the Resurrection. The principal events in the life of Christ, which may be found depicted in stained glass, follow:

The Nativity is easily recognised from the familiar elements of the stable, ox and ass, the crib with the Christchild, Mary and Joseph and angels. Often the Star is overhead; at St Peter Mancroft, Norwich, angels make a hole in the thatched roof to allow its rays to fall on the Child.

The Adoration of the Magi and Shepherds, who may be shown together, or in separate panels. The journey of the Magi and their meeting with Herod is shown in the late-twelfth-century glass at Canterbury; they are illustrated, bearing gifts, in a fine thirteenth-century medallion at Madley, Herefordshire. In the fifteenth-century glass at St Peter Mancroft, Norwich, the adoration is spread over two panels. At this church and that of East Harling, Norfolk, the adoration of the shepherds shows pipes played before the Child, who is presented with gifts of a lamb and mittens.

The Presentation at the Temple and Purification of the Virgin were rituals called for by the Jewish religion. Joseph and Mary are usually represented bringing the Child to the altar of the temple. Sometimes they bear candles and doves, part of the purification ceremony.

The Circumcision of Christ, required within eight days of birth by Jewish Law, is shown at St Peter Mancroft, Norwich, and at King's College Chapel, Cambridge, where it can be seen being carried out by a man wearing spectacles.

The Flight into Egypt is usually represented by the Virgin and Child on an ass, led by Joseph. There are early examples at Wilton, Wiltshire, and Canterbury Cathedral, and a somewhat damaged but still attractive example of the fifteenth century in the Galilee Chapel of Durham Cathedral.

The Massacre of the Innocents is illustrated by soldiers hacking babies to pieces, while their mothers plead. There is a small early fifteenth-century panel of this subject at Wormbridge, Herefordshire, and slightly later examples at Newark, Nottinghamshire, and St Peter Mancroft, Norwich, where Herod himself bisects a child with a scimitar.

Christ Disputing with the Doctors. The young Christ is shown seated in the temple before richly dressed elders with the Virgin looking on, in a panel at East Harling. At Disley, Cheshire, this scene is shown in sixteenth-century Flemish glass.

The Temptation in the Wilderness is shown in two panels from Troyes Cathedral, of 1223, now in the Victoria and Albert Museum, London. They represent Christ tempted by the devil to turn stones into bread, and being, literally, carried up to the pinnacle of the temple. The Temptation is also featured on Flemish glass of about 1525 at Southend-on-Sea, Essex.

The Miracle of the Loaves and Fishes is also shown in another panel in the same series from Troyes, at the Victoria and Albert Museum.

The Washing and Anointing of Christ's Feet by Mary Magdalene, at the house of the Pharisee, is shown in thirteenth-century glass at Canterbury and West Horsley, Surrey.

The Cleansing of the Temple appears in the early-thirteenth-century glass from France, at Wilton, Wiltshire.

The Parables are not often illustrated; that of the sower is shown in two panels of around 1200 at Canterbury Cathedral. At Melbury Bubb, the parable of the wise and foolish virgins is represented in a series of tracery lights, while a thirteenth-century medallion at Wilton shows the return of the prodigal son.

The Marriage at Cana, where Christ's first miracle, of changing water to wine, was worked, is shown at several places. An early-thirteenth-century French medallion is at Wilton, another, of the same period, is at Nackington, Kent, and a good fifteenth-century panel is in the series at East Harling.

The Miraculous Draught of Fishes is shown in the glass of about 1200 at Canterbury, where the Disciples' nets burst with fishes. This subject also occurs at Fairford.

The last events in the life of Christ, from the entry into Jerusalem to his burial, are given the collective title of the Passion. They were frequently illustrated in stained glass, and despite the depredations of earlier centuries many examples survive.

The Entry into Jerusalem. Christ is usually shown riding an ass, about to enter the city, represented as walled, with a fortified gateway. Among the places where this subject is shown are St Peter Mancroft, Norwich, Great Malvern Priory, Fairford, Gloucestershire, and St Kew, Cornwall.

Christ Washing the Disciples's feet before the Last Supper is shown at St Peter Mancroft, Norwich, and at St Kew.

The Last Supper is distinguished from the scene of the marriage feast at Cana by the absence of the winejars and women guests. At Newark, Nottinghamshire, there is an early-fourteenth-century example, where the Supper is symbolised by the figure of Christ with a piece of bread and a Disciple with a chalice. More detailed representations of the fifteenth century are at Great Malvern Priory; in a panel in the east window the Disciples and Christ are shown eating bread and fish. Judas is stealing a fish from the table. In the north transept another panel shows the same subject, but with meat on the table instead of fish.

The Agony in the Garden. The Disciples sleep in Gethsemane, while Christ prays, a little way off. This subject is portrayed in the early-fourteenth-century glass at Newark, and in late-fifteenth-century glass at Fairford and St Kew.

The Betrayal. In a Flemish panel of about 1500 at Exeter Cathedral Judas is shown receiving the thirty pieces of silver. The capture of Christ in the Garden is graphically shown at East Harling, with a panel showing Judas betraying Christ with a kiss. In the mêlée St Peter cuts off the ear of Malchus. There is a similar detail in a panel at St Kew.

Christ before Caiaphas, the High Priest, is a subject shown in a panel of the mid-sixteenth century at Southend-on-Sea, Essex. The ecclesiastical dress of the High Priest distinguishes this subject from the next.

Christ before Pilate. This scene at Disley, Cheshire, of about 1500, shows Pilate, in fashionable clothes, seated on a throne, while Christ is attended by a soldier with a spiked mace. In windows at Fairford, St Kew and East Brent, Pilate is shown washing his hands in a bowl of water.

The Scourging is shown in a number of places, including Martham, Norfolk, Disley and St Kew.

The Mocking, with Christ dressed in a robe with a crown of thorns, is illustrated at St Peter Mancroft, Norwich, in a fragmentary panel showing the crown being forced down on His head with sticks, a detail which is also shown at Great Bookham, Surrey, where His tormentors grimace and spit. At Great Malvern Priory, Christ is shown blindfolded, carrying a rush.

Ecce Home (Behold the Man). Christ is brought before the people in the robe and with the crown of thorns, by Pilate. There are sixteenth-century panels showing this scene at Disley and Southend-on-Sea.

The Road to Calvary. Christ carries the Cross, stumbling under its weight and lashed by a man with a rope, in a panel at Disley. A very stylised example of the thirteenth century is in Hereford Cathedral.

The Nailing to the Cross. In this scene, at Morley, Derbyshire, Christ's left hand is being nailed, while men stretch his arms and feet with ropes. The same scene is represented at All Saints, Pavement, York, in late-fourteenth-century glass.

The Crucifixion, central to the Christian faith, was the particular target of the iconoclasts, but despite their efforts, many examples still survive. The Crucifixion may be shown in one of several ways. The earliest forms, of the thirteenth and fourteenth centuries, are simple, with Christ on the Cross, against a plain or patterned background. The grieving figures of the Virgin and Saint John may stand on either side of the Cross, as they do in a thirteenth-century medallion at Hereford Cathedral and a fourteenth-century panel at Eaton Bishop, Herefordshire. In these early examples, the Cross is often made from green glass, to represent the living wood. The fifteenth-century panels are more detailed in most cases. At East Harling, crammed into one panel, are the Cross, the Virgin and St John, Pilate on a horse, two men, one with a bucket, and the centurion Longinus, who is saying, 'Truly this Man was the Son of God.' In the sixteenth century this scene often occupied a number of lights. In the Fairford glass, of about 1500, the same elements of the scene are spread over five lights, with the addition of the two thieves on their crosses. Over the penitent, an angel hovers, while over the impenitent, a devil waits to seize his soul. As well as these narrative representations, there are others of a more symbolic nature. At Long Melford, Suffolk, in a fifteenth-century panel, Christ is shown nailed to a lily plant, the symbol of purity and emblem of the Annunciation. At Westwood, Wiltshire, the Cross is combined with a lily plant growing from a pot. A mid- or late-sixteenth-century Flemish panel at Marston Bigot, Somerset, shows the Cross set into the bowl of a fountain, into which Christ's blood runs, pouring from spouts into a trough below. This scheme is known as 'The Fountain of Life'.

The Descent from the Cross is usually shown with the body of Christ partly detached from the Cross, supported by the Virgin and St John, as in the early-thirteenth-century panel at Twycross, Leicestershire. In this scene a man removes the nails from Christ's feet with pincers, an action also shown in the late-fourteenth-century glass at All Saints, Pavement, York.

The Pieta represents the dead Christ lying across the lap of the Virgin. At East Harling she weeps, with St John and St Mary Magdalene behind her, while in the background are the Cross and Passion symbols. At Long Melford, the body of Christ, scarred from the scourges, is wrapped by the Virgin in her red cloak.

The Deposition, or burial of Christ, displays the body lowered into a tomb, usually like a long chest. One of the earliest examples is at Rivenhall, Essex, in a French panel of about 1200. In a fourteenth-century example at All Saints, Pavement, York, Christ's body is laid on the top of a tombchest with miniature Decorated windows or arcading. At Fairford the scene is shown from an unusual angle, as if from above, as Christ is lowered into the tomb. This subject is the last of the Passion series.

The Descent into Hell. It was believed that in the three days after Christ's death on the Cross, he descended into hell to liberate the souls of mankind. In the glass at All Saints Pavement, York, He greets Adam and Eve. In the same scene at Fairford, angels armed with swords drive off demons above the gates of hell. A fragmentary panel at St Kew shows Christ leading souls out of hellmouth.

The Resurrection is illustrated by Christ, often carrying a long cross-staff with a banner, stepping out of the tomb onto or over the guardian soldiers. Often, as at East Harling, a golden radiance pours from the tomb; at Shelton a soldier is shown shielding his eyes as Christ appears.

The Two Marys at the Tomb were Mary Magdalene and Mary the mother of James, who were greeted by the angel at the empty tomb. The scene is shown at All Saints, Pavement, York, and at Fairford.

Noli Me Tangere (Touch Me Not) shows the crucified Christ's first appearance, to Mary Magdalene, in the garden. In a window at Fairford, she kneels before him, while in a somewhat faded panel at Disley, Cheshire, he carries a spade, a reference to Mary's mistaking him for a gardener.

The Road to Emmaus and the supper when Christ, unrecognised, ate with the Disciples is illustrated at Fairford.

The Unbelief of Thomas. St Thomas Didymus's demand to see and touch the Risen Christ is illustrated at All Saints, Pavement, York, where he kneels, touching Christ's side. There is a similar scene at Fairford.

The Ascension. The Disciples and the Virgin gather to watch the ascent of Christ to heaven. Usually, they look upwards at Christ's feet disappearing into a cloud. Often, Christ's footprints are shown left on the hilltop. There are good examples of this subject at East Harling and All Saints, Pavement, York.

Pentecost. Although, strictly speaking, this subject is not part of the life of Christ, it is often used as the concluding panel of a series. The composition is similar to that of the Ascension, with the Dove of the Holy Spirit descending in a radiance to the Disciples and Virgin. The East Harling window contains a good representation of this subject.

Apart from the Gospel story, there are few other subjects in the New Testament illustrated in early stained glass, although the conversion of St Paul is shown in a window at North Moreton, Berkshire. However, the last book of the New Testament, the Revelations of St John the Divine, is illustrated in great detail in the east window of York Minster. In eighty-one panels it represents St John's vision of the Apocalypse, the day of judgement when all will be held to account.

The Doom, or Last Judgement, featured frequently in medieval art, being a favourite subject for wall-paintings and often represented in stained glass. It would normally be placed in the west window, opposite the Crucifixion in the east, an arrangement which still survives at Fairford. In a typical Doom window, St Michael weighs the souls of the dead, rising naked from their tombs. Some may wear crowns or mitres to signify their earthly rank. It is interesting to note that these figures are often among those dragged by devils into the gaping jaws of hell. The blessed are conducted by angels to paradise. The most complete example, at Fairford, has already been discussed. Less complete specimens are at Ticehurst, Sussex, Tewkesbury Abbey, Gloucestershire, Thornhill, Yorkshire (a large but very faded example), and All Saints, Pavement, York. In some churches the Doom occupies the tracery of large windows, as at Selby Abbey, Yorkshire, Wells Cathedral and Chapter House, and Carlisle Cathedral, Cumberland.

The most unusual narrative window showing the end of the world is at All Saints, North Street, York. It illustrates part of a dialect poem by Richard Rolle, of Hampole, Northumberland. Rolle, born around 1290, translated parts of the Bible into English, and wrote extensively on religious matters. Part of his poem, 'The Pricke of Conscience', was based upon St Jerome's interpretation of the Book of Revelations. In fifteen panels, accompanied by a paraphrased text of the poem, the window shows the last fifteen days of the world. The glass, painted in the early fifteenth century, perhaps by John Thornton, shows such terrors as the seas burning, monsters invading the land, earthquakes, bones coming alive and the stars falling from the sky. Death at last takes all men, and the earth is destroyed by fire. In the tracery St Peter welcomes the blessed, and the damned are received by Satan and hellmouth.

The Joys and Sorrows of the Virgin Mary
In the earliest years of the Church, the Mother of Christ did not receive special veneration, but from the fifth century she began to assume greater significance and was increasingly represented in religious art. In the eleventh and twelfth centuries more legends were added to the stories in the Bible, and accounts of her birth, life and death were brought by returning crusaders and pilgrims from the Middle East. In the following two centuries she became second only to God in importance, since she was believed to intercede with her son on behalf of mankind.

The worship of the Virgin reached a peak in the fifteenth and early sixteenth centuries, during which most of the narrative windows of her life were painted. These were based on several apocryphal gospels, some of which dated back to the second century. Many of the events of her life coincide with those of Christ, described above, but there are scenes showing earlier and later events.

Joachim in the wilderness. Mary was born of rich parents, who had previously been childless for many years. As a result, Joachim, her father, was not permitted to sacrifice in the Temple. He went into the desert to fast for forty days and nights, and was visited by an angel, who comforted him. These events are shown in the glass at King's College Chapel, Cambridge, and at Gresford, Denbighshire.

The Annunciation to Anne. Joachim's wife Anne was visited by an angel, who told her she would soon bear a child, who would be blessed. This scene is distinguished from the later Annunciation to the Virgin by the greater age of Anne and the absence of the lily pot. This scene is shown at Gresford and at Great Malvern Priory, where it is set outdoors.

The Meeting at the Golden Gate. Returning from the desert, Joachim met and embraced his wife outside the city gate. It was believed that it was at this moment that the Virgin was miraculously conceived. This event is shown at Elland, Yorkshire, Gresford and King's College Chapel, and in the latter two churches the subsequent visit of the couple to the Temple is shown.

The Nativity of Mary is easily distinguished from that of Christ; the birth is set in a richly furnished interior, not a stable, and the animals, Star and so on are missing. Illustrations of this scene are in glass at the Old Jewry Museum, Leicester, and at Gresford.

St Anne Teaching the Virgin to Read is a frequently illustrated subject, shown in figure windows as well as narrative series. St Anne, dressed in the wimple and veil of a widow, points to the pages of a book while the Virgin reads. Among the many examples are those at Marsh Baldon, Oxfordshire, Almondbury and Bolton Percy, Yorkshire, Norbury, Derbyshire, Cirencester, Gloucestershire, Upper Hardres, Kent, Bere Ferrers, Devon, and Ross on Wye, Herefordshire.

The Marriage of the Virgin. Her husband, Joseph, was selected when his staff, left with those of the other unmarried men in the Temple, burst into flower, an event shown in the glass at Great Malvern Priory. Traditionally, Joseph was represented as an elderly man. The marriage ceremony is represented at King's College Chapel, Cambridge.

The Annunciation. The Archangel Gabriel appeared to the Virgin, announcing that she would miraculously conceive and give birth to Jesus. Gabriel is shown kneeling before the Virgin, who is usually at a prayer-desk. He carries a sceptre or a lily, and a lily plant is invariably present in the scene, as a symbol of purity and the emblem of the Annunciation. Often, a shaft of light falls on the Virgin, with the Dove of the Holy Spirit winging along it from heaven. Sometimes a tiny figure of the Christchild descends along the rays, as at St Peter Mancroft, Norwich. This subject is shown very often in both narrative and figure windows; among the many churches where examples can be found are Elland, Yorkshire, St Michael le

The Visitation: York school,
1501 – Great Malvern
Priory, Worcestershire

Belfrey, York, and Marston Bigot, Somerset. Often the subject occupies two adjacent tracery lights, as at Bale, Norfolk, Melbury Bubb, Dorset, and Cheddar, Somerset. It may be spread over two main lights, as occurs at Langport, Somerset, and Gresford, Denbighshire.

The Visitation to the Virgin was by Elizabeth, her cousin, who had been told by the Archangel Gabriel that, although barren, she would nonetheless conceive and give birth to John the Baptist. In the sixth month of her pregnancy she met the Virgin, an event often depicted in medieval glass. Elizabeth is shown as an older woman embracing the Virgin, or with her hand on the Virgin's stomach. At East Harling and St Peter Mancroft, Norwich, St Elizabeth is shown wearing a laced-up maternity garment. At Great Malvern Priory and Newark, Nottinghamshire, the scene is shown in glass painted at different times (1501 and around 1470) and by different artists (the Newark glass is of the York school), but they show considerable similarities of design. In both, Elizabeth touches the stomach of the Virgin, from which bursts a radiant star. Beside each figure are musical angels, and above them scrolls with appropriate texts. These similarities suggest a common source of inspiration.

There is biblical authority for the last two subjects, of course. From this point in the life of the Virgin the events are the same as those in the life of Christ, listed above. The subjects from the Nativity to Pentecost may also be shown in narrative windows of the life of the Virgin. The apocryphal gospels described later events:

[63]

The Dormition [Death] of the Virgin, where she is usually shown on her death-bed surrounded by the Apostles, who had been brought together miraculously from all over the world. It is represented in the fourteenth-century glass at North Moreton, Berkshire, and in a panel of the previous century at Woodchurch, Kent.

The Funeral of the Virgin. Her coffin, carried by the Apostles, is seized by a 'prince of the Jews' on its way to burial. His hands wither and stick to the pall. This event is shown in a fourteenth-century panel at North Moreton and one of the fifteenth century at St Peter Mancroft, Norwich. A companion panel to the latter, showing the subsequent conversion and healing of the Jew, is now in the Burrell Collection at Glasgow Art Gallery.

The Assumption of the Virgin shows her carried up to heaven by angels, and surrounded by a mandorla. There is a beautiful representation of this at East Harling, and others at Elland, Yorkshire, and North Moreton.

The Doubting of Thomas. Legend has it that St Thomas arrived too late to witness the Assumption and demanded proof, true to form. The heavens opened, and the ascending Virgin was revealed; she cast down her girdle to Thomas, whose emblem it became. He is shown with it in the east window of Gloucester Cathedral.

The Coronation of the Virgin took place in heaven after the Assumption. The seated and crowned figure of the Virgin is accompanied by that of Christ, seated on a throne and carrying an orb, divided into three parts to signify his dominion over earth, sea and sky. This subject frequently occupies two adjacent lights in tracery, as it does at Mottisfont, Hampshire, Sheering and Clavering, Essex, Stratton Strawless, Norfolk, Lanteglos by Fowey, Cornwall, Morpeth, Northumberland, West Pennard, Somerset, and Boughton Aluph, Kent, to mention only a few of the many churches in which it appears.

The Virgin is rarely shown as a single figure, although she does appear thus, holding a lily, at West Tanfield, Yorkshire. Where single figures occur, they are usually the remains of Crucifixion windows (confirmed if St John is also present), Annunciation scenes (where the prayer-desk and lily pot are indications) or of Coronation subjects (the seated pose and crown are strong clues). *The Virgin and Child* is one of the most common, yet most attractive representations of the Mother of Christ, and despite the destruction in the past many examples survive. The Virgin is usually crowned, and may carry a sceptre; often, she wears a blue robe. There are a few early examples of this subject, for instance a medallion of about 1200 at Rivenhall, Essex, of French origin, and a panel of similar age at Upper Hardres, Kent (although here the Child does not have the cross nimbus, or halo). Most examples, however, are of the fourteenth and, especially, fifteenth centuries. Sometimes the Virgin suckles the Child, as at York Minster, Cartmel Priory, Lancashire, Fladbury, Worcestershire, and Yarnton, Oxfordshire. The Child may carry flowers, as he does at Martham, Norfolk, and St Winnow, Cornwall. Often, he holds a pear, as shown at Fladbury, Wormbridge, Herefordshire, Ringland and North Elmham in Norfolk. At Wooley, Yorkshire, Jesus reaches for the fruit held by the Virgin. He may hold a bird, shown at St Paul's Walden, Hertfordshire, Northleach and Cirencester, Gloucestershire, Buckland, Surrey, and Eaton Bishop, Herefordshire. At Attleborough, Norfolk, he has a bird in one hand and a pear in the other.

'Virgin and Child', first half of the fourteenth century – Fladbury, Worcestershire

[64]

Left : 'St Catherine', *c.* 1320
Deerhurst, Gloucestershire
right : 'St John the Baptist'
mid-fourteenth century –
Grappenhall, Cheshire

S:CATHERINE

The Holy Families
Sometimes the family of the Virgin Mary is shown with those of the other Marys –
Mary Salome and Mary Cleophas. The Virgin is usually shown with the Christchild and accompanied by her parents Anne and Joachim. Mary Salome, the
mother of Sts James and John, is shown with her husband Zebedee. Mary
Cleophas is represented with her husband Alpheus and the future saints, her
children Jude, Simeon, James the less and Joseph Barsabus. The children may
carry toy versions of their emblems as saints. There are complete sets of the Holy
Families at Thornhill, Yorkshire, and Holy Trinity, Goodramgate, York.

The Representations of God
The Three Persons of the Trinity may be shown singly, or as three identical
figures, or as a combination of the three figures.

Christ can be always distinguished from other holy figures by the nimbus with a
cross. He may appear as a single figure, as well as in narrative panels. Shown
enthroned, with the orb of the world in His hand, in majesty, He is usually a
surviving figure from a Coronation of the Virgin subject.

The Risen Christ is shown as a partly clothed figure, carrying a long cross-staff
with a cross-banner. One hand may be held up in blessing, and the wounds in
hands and feet are usually clearly visible. In the sixteenth-century glass at
Rendcombe, Gloucestershire, He is accompanied by a scroll with the inscription
in English, 'I go to prepare a place for you'. This subject also appears at Wooley,
Yorkshire, and All Saints, North Street, York. In this scheme, He is not accompanied by the tomb or soldiers.

Christ Showing His Wounds. He stands, both hands raised, displaying the wounds
in his palms; usually he wears the crown of thorns. He is shown thus at Weston
Underwood, Buckinghamshire. This pose was often used as the centrepiece of a
Seven Sacraments windows, as at Melbury Bubb, Dorset, and Crudwell,
Wiltshire.

God the Father is usually shown as a bearded, venerable figure, with the cross-
nimbus. At Atcham, Shropshire, he has one hand raised in blessing, and carries a
chalice. In narrative windows of the Creation, he is shown normally as an old man,
as at Great Malvern Priory; at St Neot, Cornwall, however, the Creator is drawn
to look more like Christ.

God the Holy Spirit is represented as a white Dove with outspread wings; it
appears thus in a window head at Willesborough, Kent. There is a cross-nimbus
about its head. The Holy Spirit appears in scenes of the Annunciation and Pentecost. In the latter subject, at Fairford, the Dove is surrounded by a white radiance,
from a distance giving the effect of a white-robed figure.

The Trinity may be shown in one of several ways. Most common is that where God
the Father is seated, supporting the crucified Christ, above whose head the Dove
hovers. Where the Cross is present, it may rest upon the orb of the world. There
are examples at All Saints, North Street, and Holy Trinity, Goodramgate, York,
Ringland, Thurton and South Creake, Norfolk, Wooley, Yorkshire, Orchardleigh,

Somerset, Mottisfont, Hampshire, and Bilsington, Kent. At All Saints, Pavement, York, the Dove perches on the shoulder of God, while at Ludlow, Shropshire, God the Father holds a diminutive figure of Christ in his hands. The Trinity may be represented as three identical figures: at Holy Trinity, Goodramgate, York, the three elderly figures wear papal tiaras. One has a young boy before him, for God the Son, one holds a cross-nimbed Dove, for God the Holy Spirit, and the centre figure carries an orb and sceptre, for God the Father. At Doddiscombleigh there are three purple-robed, crowned and bearded figures with yellow faces, representing the Trinity.

The representations of the Three Persons in stained glass were particular targets for destruction. The heads of a very large number of the surviving figures of Christ are missing, or are modern restorations. Such replacements are usually obvious, sometimes painfully so.

Religious symbols and emblems

Among the symbols representing abstract religious concepts to be found in stained glass is that of the *Pelican in her Piety*. The pelican was believed to feed her young on her own blood, and was thus seen as a symbol of Christ's atonement on the Cross, and man's redemption. It is illustrated by the pelican (not drawn to resemble the bird we know) pecking at its own breast, surrounded by its young. It is shown thus at Pendomer, Somerset, and Beverley Minster, Yorkshire.

The symbol of the *Trinity* is a shield, bearing in its centre a circle with the inscription 'Deus' (God). It is joined by three inscriptions 'est' (is) to three circles, two above and one below, marked 'Pater' (Father), 'Filius' (Son) and 'Spiritus Sanctus' (Holy Ghost). In turn, these are connected to each other by inscriptions 'non est' (is not). Thus the shield symbolises the separate nature of the Three Persons and their simultaneous unity in God. It is in stained glass at Newark, Nottinghamshire, Mark, Somerset, Gazeley, Suffolk, and Greystoke, Cumberland.

The letters IHC or IHS are the first three of the Greek name of Jesus; as his symbol they are shown in glass at Orchardleigh, Swell and Trull, in Somerset, filling tracery lights. The letter M is the sign of the Virgin Mary. It may appear as a border motif, as at Taverham, Norfolk, around a figure of the Virgin. At Bale, Norfolk, it is used to decorate her robe.

The *Agnus Dei*, a lamb bearing a cross-staff and banner, is another symbol of Christ, the Lamb of God. As such, it is carried by John the Baptist as his emblem. It is often represented on its own; there is an early-thirteenth-century example at Hereford Cathedral, and one of the fifteenth century at North Cadbury, Somerset. At Stratton Strawless, Norfolk, the banner reads 'Ecce Agnus Dei' – Behold the Lamb of God.

The emblems of the Four Evangelists have been mentioned already: the angel of St Matthew, the winged lion of St Mark, the winged ox of St Luke and the eagle of St John. There are complete sets of these emblems at Doddiscombleigh, Devon, Great Malvern Priory, Hereford Cathedral, Trull and Cheddar, Somerset, Attleborough, Norfolk, and Canterbury Cathedral.

The *Passion Symbols* are represented on shields, usually supported by angels. They include the following: scourges and scourging post, crown of thorns, spear with sponge, lantern, pestle and mortar, spitting Jew, money-bag or pieces of silver, a hand pulling hair, pierced heart, ladder, reed, seamless shirt and dice, hammer, pincers, nails, a striking hand and, of course, the Cross. There are large sets at Westwood, Wiltshire, Winscombe, Somerset, and Laneast, Cornwall.

Other examples are at Butcombe, Ditcheat and Leigh on Mendip, Somerset, Great Malvern Priory, Worcestershire, and Poringland, Norfolk. Sometimes a number of symbols are combined on a single shield, as at Gazeley, Suffolk, Kingsbury Episcopi and Mark, Somerset, Sherbourne Hospital, Dorset, Newark, Nottinghamshire, and Woodton, Norfolk. As will be seen from the places mentioned, the Passion symbols are especially common in west-country churches.

Religious rites and devotional subjects

One of the most interesting 'set pieces' of fifteenth-century stained glass was that of the *Seven Sacraments*. Seven panels showing the sacraments of the Church were arranged around a figure of Christ, on the Cross or showing his wounds, to which the sacrament panels may be connected by red lines. No such window survives intact, although at Doddiscombleigh, Devon, the complete series is arranged around a Victorian figure of Christ. At the Old Jewry Museum, Leicester, the sacraments survive in glass of the early sixteenth century. The scenes shown are similar in both series:

Baptism. A priest prepares to immerse the naked baby in the font, while members of the family touch its head.

Confirmation. At Doddiscombleigh a bishop is shown blessing a tiny child, held by a man; behind, a woman stands with a baby bound in the chrysom cloth. An acolyte holds the Chrismatory, a holy oil casket. At Leicester the bishop confirms a child wrapped in the chrysom cloth, while behind, a woman suckles her child. Confirmation was carried out on very young children in the middle ages, and they were kept in the chrysom cloth until they had been anointed with the holy oil.

Penance. A red-robed and cowled monk sits at a 'shriving pew' in the Doddiscombleigh window, reading from a book and blessing a kneeling penitent. At Leicester the cleric sits on a throne-like chair.

Mass or Eucharist. In the Doddiscombleigh subject, the priest elevates the Host before an altar with a statue of the Virgin and Child. The congregation kneel behind him, and an acolyte holds a sanctuary bell on a staff. The Leicester panel is similar, but less detailed.

Extreme Unction or Communion of the Sick. The latter subject is shown at Doddiscombleigh, with a priest delivering the Host from a paten to a sick man in bed. Acolytes carry a candle and the Pyx, used to carry the consecrated Host. At Leicester the priest administers extreme unction.

Ordination. Three priests kneel before a bishop, who lays his hands on the tonsured head of one of them. Behind, acolytes hold a book and the chrismatory. At Leicester the priests are standing, and the bishop holds the hand of one of them.

Matrimony. The priest holds the wrists of the couple as the ring is placed on the bride's finger. At Leicester fashionably dressed guests look on.

There are remains of Sacraments windows at a number of places. They include Bishop's Lydeard, Somerset (baptism), Buckland, Gloucestershire (marriage, ordination and confirmation), Durham Cathedral (marriage), Melbury Bubb, Dorset (ordination), Crudwell, Wiltshire (ordination, baptism, penance, extreme unction and marriage), Cartmell Fell, Lancashire (mass, communion of the sick and marriage), Tattershall, Lincolnshire (baptism, confirmation), and Llandrynog, Denbighshire (ordination, marriage and extreme unction).

The Seven Corporal Acts of Mercy were based upon Christ's words given in Matthew 25, verses 35–50:

> 'For I was an hungred, and ye gave me meat: I was thirsty, and ye gave me drink: I was a stranger and ye took me in: Naked, and ye clothed me: I was sick, and ye visited me: I was in prison, and ye came unto me . . . Inasmuch as ye have done it unto one of the least of my brethren, ye have done it unto me.'

To the six merciful acts mentioned by Christ was added another, burial of the dead, to make up the mystical number seven. The most complete set of this subject is at All Saints, North Street, York, where the six acts mentioned in the Bible are illustrated. Five of the seven are represented in roundels now in the Old Jewry Museum at Leicester.

Feeding the Hungry. At All Saints a richly dressed benefactor, helped by a servant in particoloured hose, dispenses loaves of bread from a large basket. At Leicester only the basket and part of the donor survive from this scene.

Drink to the Thirsty. In the All Saints glass, the benefactor pours from a ewer into drinking bowls, while the servant stands by with more jugs and bowls. Among the crowd is a kneeling cripple with hand crutches. This subject is shown in the glass at Leicester.

Shelter to the Stranger. The benefactor greets pilgrims at the door of his house; one leads a blind man by a looped cord.

Clothing the Naked. A small crowd of men, wearing undergarments only, receive clothing from the benefactor. At Leicester the donor helps one dress.

Visiting the sick. The benefactor stands at the sick man's bedside, placing money on the bed, while the wife looks on. This scene is shown at both All Saints and Leicester.

Visiting the Prisoners is shown at All Saints. The benefactor brings food and drink to three men fettered and in the stocks. He is reaching for money in his purse, while a jailor or constable looks on.

Burying the Dead is shown at Leicester only. A body in a shroud is lowered into a grave, while a priest with a cross-staff sprinkles holy water. An acolyte holds a candle, while another carries an open book. In the foreground are bones and a spade.

There are remains of Acts of Mercy windows at Combs, Suffolk (feeding the hungry, giving drink to the thirsty), Chinnor, Oxfordshire (clothing the naked, giving drink to the thirsty), and Tattershall, Lincolnshire (clothing the naked and feeding the hungry).

The Seven Deadly Sins appear only once in surviving stained glass, and then only in an incomplete set, at Newark, Nottinghamshire. Those surviving are:
Anger. A man holds a knife, with his other hand crooked with rage.

Gluttony. A man holds a leg of meat and a drinking bowl; a jug hangs from his belt.
Lust. A couple embrace.
Pride or Hypocrisy. A man, with a superior expression, ostentatiously prays.
Avarice. Fragments remain of a man with money-bags.
The remaining sins, *envy* and *sloth*, are missing. Chains surrounding the figures

suggest that they might once have been shown being dragged by demons into hell.

The Seven Cardinal Virtues complement and counterbalancé the Deadly Sins. Four of the Virtues are shown in the early glass of about 1178 in the Rose window of the north-east transept of Canterbury Cathedral. They are *Justice*, with scales, *Temperance*, with a bowl of water, *Fortitude*, with a sword, and *Prudence*, with a dove and winged serpent. Virtues are also represented in the medieval glass at Tattershall, Lincolnshire.

The Ten Commandments. Six are illustrated at Ludlow, Shropshire. In each case, Moses is shown holding the tables of the Law, inscribed with the appropriate Commandment. Above him is shown one of the Three Persons of the Trinity or an angel. Below, figures illustrate the Commandment:
Thou shalt not kill. A small figure kneels before a bearded man.
Thou shalt not commit adultery. A couple embrace and kiss.
Thou shalt not steal. A thief cuts the purse from a rich man's belt.
Thou shalt not bear false witness. A king, with upraised hands, is shown.
Thou shalt not covet thy neighbour's wife. A man with a sensual face looks at a woman.
Thou shalt not covet thy neighbour's house. Soldiers besiege a castle, and at the gate an engineer blows at a fire with bellows.

The Mystery Plays

Before ending this outline of the religious imagery of medieval stained glass, something must be said of the influence of early religious drama. The earliest dramatisations were by priests, who began to act out parts of the liturgy in the chancel of the church, in order to better communicate with a largely illiterate congregation. Later, the Gospel story was shown in simple dramatisations in the nave and chancel, especially at Easter time. At Rivenhall, Essex, a French medallion of about 1200 shows the Deposition of the dead Christ. A sanctury lamp hangs above the tombchest, and it is possible that the glazier's inspiration was drawn from a representation of this subject in dramatic form in the chancel of the church. As the dramatic presentations became more elaborate, they were moved outside the church and became mobile, with stages and scenery mounted on carts. The more complex presentations involved the laity as well as the priests, and finally the plays were taken over and administered by the trade and religious guilds. They were presented on feast days, particularly Corpus Christi. With their crude but vivid characterisations and comic 'business' they would have been familiar to the glass-painter and the churchgoer, and they clearly influence the representations of biblical scenes in stained glass and other religious art.

For example, the serpent, in the story of the temptation of Adam and Eve, was played by an actor whose head showed above scenery on which the snake's body was painted, rather in the manner of the seaside photographer's comic props. In stained-glass pictures of this subject, the serpent almost invariably has a human head, as it does in the Creation window at St Neot, Cornwall, which illustrates the Creation in a similar way to the fourteenth-century Cornish mystery play *Origo Mundi*. In particular, there is a scene in both the play and the window where Adam on his deathbed sends his son Seth to paradise, to discover whether he will be allowed to return. Through the gates, Seth sees a great tree, with a Child in its branches. Seth is given by an angel three pips from the apple which led to the fall of man and is instructed to place them under Adam's tongue, when he dies.

From those pips, it was said, grew the tree on which Christ was crucified, and through which Adam and his descendants could at last return to paradise.

There were distinct changes in the representation of the Resurrection between the fourteenth and fifteenth centuries. In the earlier glass, the soldiers guarding the tomb are often shown asleep, or perhaps, as St Matthew said, they 'became as dead men'. In the fifteenth-century plays, the soldiers had lines to speak and actions to perform, and this is clearly illustrated in the narrative windows by their attitudes of fear in response to the figure of the Risen Christ, who is often shown stepping on one of the soldiers as he leaves the tomb – surely a piece of stage management. Where there was little information in the biblical story of, say, the Nativity, extra characters would be introduced, such as the midwives mentioned in an apocryphal second-century gospel. Two are shown in the Nativity Panel at East Harling, as they were represented in the Coventry Corpus Christi mystery play, and there are other indications that the painter of this window was familiar with the drama. The Coventry Shearmen and Taylor's play included the lines by the first shepherd:

Hayle Maid Mother and wife so mild,
As the angel said, so have we found.
I have nothing to present with this Chylde
But my pype; hold, hold, take yt in thi hand
Wherein much pleasure that I have found.

In the East Harling panel, the shepherd is shown playing the double hornpipe, while his companions present mittens and a lamb, both mentioned in the drama.

The feathered costume worn by the actors representing angels has already been mentioned; the creation of the Nine Orders of Angels began many of the play cycles, and the distinctive costumes worn by the actors undoubtedly influenced the representations of angels in fifteenth-century glass. At St Michael, Spurriergate, York, angels are shown wearing belts of spherical 'jingle' bells, which must be a reference to a costume detail from a play.

The scenes showing souls being wheeled to hell by devils using handcarts and wheelbarrows, as at Fairford, surely must have been based upon comic 'business' by the actors in the early plays.

5

THE SECULAR CONTENT

THE primary purpose of creating images in stained glass was a religious one. We can be sure that the glass-painter and his customer were not consciously recording the way they looked and lived for posterity. Yet this is what they did. Through the small fraction of stained glass which has survived, we can still learn much about our ancestors of over four hundred years ago. It is true that other sources, notably illuminated manuscripts, give far more variety and detail, but for the amateur they are not readily accessible. Happily, most churches are still freely open to the serious student of medieval life and art. In this chapter the secular content of the stained-glass window will be considered.

Heraldry

The origins of heraldry are obscure, but it is known to have developed as a science during the Crusades, and had certainly appeared in a recognisable and organised form by the beginning of the third Crusade, around 1190. By the middle of the thirteenth century it was a fully developed system, and the oldest rolls of arms – accounts of the heraldry of named individuals – date from this period. The first heraldic stained glass was made soon after, around 1270. Since the language of heraldry is based on Norman French, it is sometimes difficult for the beginner to understand, although the basic rules are simple enough. At the risk of offending the specialist the precise, but (for the beginner) obscure terminology used by the herald will not be used here, except where there is no commonplace equivalent. The reader is urged to learn more of this intriguing subject, since a knowledge of heraldry can be useful in identifying and dating ancient glass.

The shield is the basis of heraldic display. The shape varies from the almost triangular, in the thirteenth and fourteenth centuries, to almost square, or very irregular, in the sixteenth century. Whatever the shape, the principles governing the display on the shield are the same. The surface of the shield may be represented in several ways. There are two heraldic metals, gold (or) and silver (argent). In glass these are shown by yellow and white respectively. Next there are five principal colours, blue (azure), red (gules), black (sable), green (vert) and purple (purpure), shown by glass of the appropriate colour. Finally there are furs, of which the two most common are ermine (black spots on white) and vair, or squirrel-fur (bell shapes, alternately coloured blue and white, and arranged in rows). Although there are other colours and furs in heraldry, they need not concern us since they are rarely seen in stained glass. Normally the field or surface of the shield is in one metal or colour only, but it may be arranged in alternate squares of metal and colour. The chequée field, as it is called, is familiar from the arms of de

Warrenne, where the field is chequered with blue and gold squares. The influence of the de Warrennes was widespread, and many an inn called The Chequers owes its name to a local branch of the family. The de Warrenne arms can be seen in churches all over the country, for instance at Dewsbury, Yorkshire, Church Leigh, Staffordshire, Madley, Herefordshire, and Selling, Kent.

The field may be divided in several ways; for example, vertically into halves (per pale), horizontally into halves (per fesse) or both (quarterly). These divisions may be continued so as to divide the shield into many compartments, a feature of later heraldic glass. When the arms of two families were combined, the shield could be divided vertically and the arms of the two families displayed on either side, a method known as impaling. Alternatively, the arms could be combined by quartering, with the two displays repeated in opposite corners.

Upon the field, be it metal, colour or fur, can be placed charges, devices which can range from simple geometric figures to detailed representations of natural objects or symbols. These must be thought of as being applied to and covering part of the field. There is a firm heraldic rule: a coloured charge is never placed on a coloured field, or a metal on a metal. Metals are placed on colours, and vice versa. Occasionally, this rule may seem to be broken in heraldic stained glass; if so, it is always due to error, limitations of technique or faulty repair. The rule does not apply to field colours on divided shields, since these are not *on* each other, but side by side in the same plane.

There is practically no limit to the variety of objects or shapes that may be used as charges in heraldry. There are a number of simple shapes, known as ordinaries to the herald, which appear on early shields. They are: the *chief*, a horizontal strip across the top third of the shield; the *fesse*, a horizontal strip across the middle third; the *bar*, a narrow horizontal strip placed elsewhere; the *pale*, a vertical strip down the centre third of the shield; the *cross*, a combination of the fesse and pale. Heraldic crosses appear in many varieties, usually distinguished by the terminations of the arms, each with its own term; the *bend*, a diagonal strip crossing the shield from top left to bottom right; the *saltire*, a Saint Andrew's cross formed by a bend combined with a similar strip running from top right to bottom left; the *chevron*, an upside-down V-shape; the *pile*, a wedge-shape, point downward, from the top to the bottom of the shield.

These charges, in some instances, can be shown in diminutive forms, and they can be repeated. Their edges can be straight, wavy, toothed, or dovetailed, and other charges can be placed upon them, subject only to the rule governing the use of metals and colours. Thus it will be seen that there is an almost infinite range of combinations so that no two people of different family need bear the same coat of arms.

Apart from these simple geometric shapes, other charges might be derived from the animal kingdom. The most familiar example is of the three gold lions on a red field, the arms of England. The lions are said to be *passant-guardant*, that is to say shown walking to the left with their heads turned towards the observer. Another common pose for the heraldic lion is *rampant*, standing on its hind legs as if clawing the air. It is the charge of the de Mowbray family, in silver on a red field, and of the Percy family, whose lion is blue on a golden field. Examples of both can be seen in heraldic glass at Holy Trinity, Goodramgate, York. Among the various heraldic birds is the martlet, a martin shown in profile. It features in a number of coats of arms, notably those of the Lutterel family, whose shield can be seen in glass at Pitcombe, Somerset. The martlet also appears on the arms attributed to Edward the Confessor, long after his death. The arms, a cross and five martlets in gold on a blue field, are impaled with the attributed arms of King Edmund (three gold crowns on a blue field) in heraldic glass at Westwell, Kent. Flowers and plants are another common source of charges. The arms of Sir Thomas de Bradestone bear a golden rose in a red canton – a square in the top left-hand corner – of a silver shield. It is shown in the window he donated at Gloucester Cathedral.

Items of dress have been used as charges. The *manche* is an heraldic representation of the sleeve of a lady's dress, with a long, hanging cuff. It is shown in the arms of the de Mauley family, in red on vair, in the window they donated to York Minster. Crowns feature in the previously mentioned arms of King Edmund, and these are represented at Gazeley, Suffolk. Household and everyday articles sometimes feature as heraldic charges. Water bougets, the water-carrying devices used by the Crusaders, in heraldry resemble rather fat upturned commas linked by a rod. They were the charges of the de Ros family, appearing in silver on a red ground, and shown in several churches, including Well, Yorkshire, and Holy Trinity, Goodramgate, York. A gold disc, the bezant, is said to have been a representation of the gold coins of Byzantium, used by the Crusaders. A notable family, the de la Zouches, had nine gold bezants on a blue field, as shown in arms at Stottesdon, Shropshire.

Perhaps the most interesting are the arms which are visual puns, or direct illustrations of the bearer's name. The Montacute arms of three red lozenges on a silver field are a symbolic reference to *mont acute*, a sharply pointed mountain. They can be seen, impaling those of Grandisson, in Exeter Cathedral. The arms of Lord Ferrers, at Bere Ferrers, Devon, carry three silver horseshoes on a black bend, on a gold field; a reference to the French *ferreur*, a shoeing smith. Three silver fish on a red field are the arms of de Lucy, seen quartered with the arms of Percy at Bolton Percy, Yorkshire. The connection becomes apparent when we learn that the fishes now called pikes were called lucies in medieval times. More obvious, the arms of Sir Robert Wingfield, at East Harling, Norfolk, display three pairs of wings in silver on a red bend and silver field. There is no doubt at all of the origin of the arms of John Gunthorpe, Dean of Wells. Shown in glass at Mark, Somerset, they carry three black guns with a red chevron on a silver field. The arms of Beare, at St Kew, Cornwall, are as plain as can be – a black bear on a silver field.

The Royal arms, as one might expect, appear frequently in medieval glass, and examples are found in the oldest heraldic glass to survive, at Salisbury Cathedral and Chetwode, Buckinghamshire, although in the latter church the lions are reversed. The lion was first used as a Royal badge by King Henry I, during whose reign a lion was said to have been brought to England. It is believed that he added a second to his badge on his marriage to the daughter of Godfrey of Louvain in 1121. His son, Henry II, added a third lion on his marriage to Eleanor of Aquitaine, whose arms were a single gold lion on a red field. The first representation of the three passant-guardant lions is on the seal of his son, Richard I. They have remained part of the Royal arms ever since. From about 1190 to 1340 the arms of England were the three lions passant guardant in gold on a red field. Examples can be seen at Selling, Kent, Madley, Herefordshire, Holy Trinity, Goodramgate, York, and Stottesdon, Shropshire. In 1340 Edward III declared himself King of France, and quartered the French arms – gold fleurs-de-lis scattered on a blue field – with those of England. The 'new' arms can be seen in glass at Gloucester and Canterbury Cathedrals. Around 1405, when the French arms were changed to just three gold lilies, the English Royal arms were altered accordingly, since

Henry IV claimed sovereignty over France. The changed arms are included in glass at Canterbury Cathedral, Thirsk, Yorkshire, and elsewhere. There was no change in the Royal arms until 1603, when they were combined with those of Ireland and Scotland. In Tudor times the Royal arms were usually supported by a red dragon and silver greyhound, as at Canterbury Cathedral and Newark, Nottinghamshire, or by the red dragon and golden lion, as shown at Nynehead, Somerset, and Canterbury Cathedral. In the two latter cases, the arms were surrounded by the Garter. At King's College Chapel, Cambridge, the Tudor arms are shown on a flag carried by a red dragon.

The arms of the eldest son of the monarch were distinguished during the king's lifetime by a mark of cadency. This was a *label*, a device rather like the letter E turned on its side, but sometimes bearing more than three points. It was placed over the other charges at the top of the shield. The sons of Henry III and Edward I and II bore a blue label over the Royal arms, as at Ripon Cathedral and Gloucester Cathedral, where the label has the gold fleurs-de-lis of France added to it, for the Earl of Lancaster. Edward, the Black Prince, adopted a silver label on the new Royal arms, and this has remained the mark of cadency for the succeeding Princes of Wales. The Black Prince's arms are shown at Gloucester Cathedral, while examples of the later Royal arms with the label are in glass at Sherborne Abbey, Dorset, and Little Malvern, Worcestershire.

In addition to the full display of arms, heraldic badges are seen in glass, often in borders or window heads. Sometimes the motifs are derived from the coat of arms, but may also be additional signs of recognition. Many Royal badges appear in stained glass. Edward II, reigning from 1307 to 1327, adopted a castle, from his mother Eleanor of Castile, and golden castles are a common border motif in the early fourteenth century. They are shown in the glass at St Denys, York, Merton College Chapel, Oxford, and Credenhill, Herefordshire. In the latter two churches, and elsewhere, the castle is associated with the fleur-de-lis, adopted as a badge by Edward III (1327–77). The Sun in Splendour had been used by Richard II (1377–99), but was the particular badge of Edward IV (1461–83). It appears in many windows in the later fifteenth century; an interesting example is shown in the Corpus Christi window in All Saints, North Street, York, where it is displayed on a banner carried by one of the participants. Edward had also adopted the white rose, as Henry IV (1399–1413) had the red (shown in the glass at Yeovilton, Somerset). Henry VII (1485–1509) combined the red and white roses and adopted the portcullis, and both were retained by his son Henry VIII (1509–47). Good examples of both badges are shown at Nynehead, Somerset.

The three ostrich feathers first adopted by the Black Prince have been associated with the Prince of Wales ever since. They are shown in the background to the figure of Edward, Prince of Wales, in the window of around 1480 in the north-west transept of Canterbury Cathedral. Edmund Langley, Duke of York and son of Edward III, took as his badge a closed fetterlock, symbolising the locking away of his line from the throne by Henry Bolingbroke. It is shown in the glass at Hunsdon, Hertfordshire, together with a white rose. At Canterbury Cathedral, as a background to the figure of Richard, Duke of York, open fetterlocks, enclosing the Langley falcon, are shown, symbolising the restoration to the throne of the Yorkist line with the accession of Edward IV in 1461. A badge of three daisies on a grass tuft, the badge of Lady Margaret, Countess of Richmond and mother of Henry VII, is shown on quarries surrounding figures at St Winnow, Cornwall, and around a Crucifixion at Durham Cathedral. The supporters of the rival houses of Lancaster and York displayed their allegiance by wearing collars with badges. The

Lancastrian collar bore the letter S repeated, said to have been derived from Henry IV's motto 'Souveraine'. It is worn by Sir Thomas Ashton, at Ashton under Lyne, Lancashire. The Yorkist collar carried alternate suns and roses, and is clearly shown on the figure of Sir Robert Wingfield, at East Harling, Norfolk. Much of the political history of the Middle Ages can be illustrated by the heraldic devices in stained-glass windows, and they can be of help in dating the glass with which they are associated.

Badges representing many other families are illustrated in glass. The bear and ragged staff (a lopped treetrunk) of the Beauchamp family, Earls of Warwick, is a famous example. In John Prudde's glass at Warwick the bear and the staff are shown separately; elsewhere they are combined, with the bear chained to the tree. The signs of less illustrious families can also be found in medieval glass. The badge of John Heron, Portreeve of Langport, Somerset, was, unsurprisingly, a heron, and is shown in the east window of Langport church. The Lovell badge, a red squirrel, is placed in the tracery of the east window of East Harling church, Norfolk. Some of the foreign glass now in England contains illustrations of heraldic badges. The flint and steel badge of the Order of the Golden Fleece is depicted on the costume of a figure in a Flemish panel now in the Victoria and Albert Museum, London.

Costume and armour

For the student of costume, stained glass can provide a valuable source of information, supplementing that derived from a study of monumental brasses and effigies. Indeed, the author's own enthusiasm for stained glass was aroused through an interest in costume and armour pursued through brass rubbing. Stained glass shows many aspects of costume not covered by the memorial sculpture – clothing of the poor, working clothes, nightwear and so on. The clothes are shown in colour, often from the side or rear, giving details not often shown on brasses. Few brasses survive from before 1300, and although there are earlier carved effigies, they are mostly of armoured figures. Stained glass is thus a particularly useful source of information about early medieval civilian costume, even though the surviving glass is often fragmentary. For the purpose of this book only the main changes of costume, which may help to date the glass, will be discussed. For more detailed explanations of the evolution of medieval dress the reader is referred to the sources given in the bibliography.

It must be understood that the medieval artist had virtually no knowledge of the history of costume and painted figures in the dress with which he was familiar. Only with the revival of interest in antiquity during the Renaissance was any attempt made to show more archaic costume. Regardless of the person shown, the costume worn is roughly contemporary with the period in which the glass was painted. Thus, Noah is dressed like a wealthy fifteenth-century merchant in the window at St Neot, Cornwall, and St George may be shown in the armour of the fourteenth century, as he is at Wells Cathedral.

The Trinity Chapel and choir aisle windows of Canterbury Cathedral provide the main source of information on late-twelfth- and thirteenth-century costume in stained glass. During this period the standard male dress was a tunic, usually belted, and often reaching to the ankles. A cloak, normally fastened at one shoulder, was generally worn. The baggy loose drawers worn as underclothing are shown in some of the panels in the Trinity Chapel windows. The most common footwear were pointed-toed shoes or buskins reaching up to the calf. Long hose were worn and in a panel showing trial by combat the characters have cross-gartering over their stockings. This had gone out of fashion by about 1100, but was enjoying a brief revival of popularity around 1200, just before the glass was painted. Few of the figures in the Canterbury glass wear head-dress, except for the official head coverings worn by kings and ecclesiastics. However, some of the late-twelfth-century figures in the south-west transept window at Canterbury wear coifs or skull-caps.

The figure of Aram, of around 1190, in the Trinity Chapel west window has a hat rather like an upturned funnel, and other figures in the same window wear the beret-like cap with a stalk, usually associated with doctors or philosophers. Women's dress closely resembles that of the men at this time. They wear long gowns or kirtles, with a girdle at the waist, and mantles reaching to the ground. Their shoes are pointed, like those of the men. Head-dress and hair styles provide the most accurate clues for dating glass of this and later periods. The barbette was typical of the thirteenth century, and was a band of linen passing under the chin and over the head, pinned at the top. A fillet of stiffened linen was usually worn round the head, like a crown. A veil was commonly worn, covering the head and hanging down over the shoulders. It can be seen in a thirteenth-century figure of the Virgin at Church Leigh, Staffordshire, and in many of the panels of the Trinity Chapel windows at Canterbury, where the end of the veil is often wound round the neck like a scarf. The wimple was a length of silk or linen covering the neck and breast, with the ends pulled up to surround the face. When a veil was worn as well, only a small triangle of the face was visible. An early example is shown in the glass at Nackington, Kent. The hair was rarely shown, except on figures of unmarried girls and the Virgin. After around 1270 the hair was plaited and rolled on either side of the head, held in a crespine or hairnet.

There was no change in men's costume until around 1335, when the gipon began to replace the tunic. It was a shaped garment following closely the contours of the body, and reaching almost to the knees at first, but becoming longer as time went on. Buttons or laces were used to fasten the front. An example can be seen in fourteenth-century glass at Appleby Magna, Leicestershire. Over the gipon a cote-hardie was worn, a long-sleeved garment which could be short and cape-like or full length. From 1380 a new form of gown was worn, the houpelande, of knee or ankle length, with a high, stiff collar and very wide sleeves. Examples can be seen in the glass at All Saints, North Street, York. Until the end of the fourteenth century the cloak might also be worn. Women's dress also changed in style around 1330. Like the male equivalent, the kirtle was now cut to the figure, with a lower neckline and long buttoned sleeves. A cote-hardie similar to that of the men, and also closely fitting, was worn over the kirtle. A sideless surcoat, with openings from the shoulders to the hips, was also in fashion from the beginning of the fourteenth century. The veil, often held in place with a fillet, continued in use, as did the wimple. There is a good example on the figure of St Anne, at Marsh Baldon, Oxfordshire. It became unfashionable from around 1340 except for widows, for whom it was standard dress. In the early years of the century the barbette and fillet were still worn, as they are shown on the figure of St Anne at Bere Ferrers, Devon, but as time went on, the barbette was omitted and the hair was massed round the ears. From 1340 the hair was arranged in vertical plaits on either side of the face. After 1350 the veil became more elaborate, a semicircle of linen with a goffered frill like a ruff at the front crowning the head. The plain remainder of the veil hung down to the shoulders. The frill was sometimes extended down either side of the face, enclosing it in a square arch of goffered linen, perhaps covered with an ornamental net. The wife of Richard Toller, in a panel in the north transept of York Minster, has this head-dress, with a wimple. The pointed shoes continued in fashion for men and women, although after 1360 men's shoes began to have much longer toes, a fashion that became very extravagant at the end of the century.

In the fifteenth century, costume is shown in more detail, and there are many more examples to be found in stained glass. The gipon continued in fashion, but became known as the doublet. At first it was a little more than hip length, but became much shorter by the end of the century. Initially it had no collar, but after 1420 close-fitting collars were added, becoming high with a V-front after the middle of the century. Several examples are shown on the figures in the Jesse Tree at Margaretting, Essex. The houpelande was still worn, often fur-trimmed and with baggy sleeves; one is shown on the figure of Richard Stowting, at Stowting, Kent. After the middle of the century the jacket came into fashion, replacing the côte-hardie, and worn over the doublet. It was high-waisted, with heavily padded shoulders. With the fashion for shorter clothes, hose appear more often in stained glass. The separate stockings were replaced by tights around 1400; an attractively decorated pair is shown in a Labours of the Month roundel at the Victoria and Albert Museum, London. The legs of the tights were sometimes of different colours, as is shown in the Acts of Mercy window at All Saints, North Street, York. After 1410 the codpiece became fashionable, formed by a flap at the front of the fork of the hose. An example can be seen on the figure of a mower in a Labours of the Months roundel at Checkley, Staffordshire. The shoes became less pointed, and were more like short boots, covering the ankle and fastened with buttons or buckles. They are shown clearly in an Acts of Mercy panel at the Old Jewry Museum, Leicester, and at Marston Bigot, Somerset. The buskin, or calf-length boot, often had a turned-over top, as shown in the glass at St Peter Mancroft, Norwich. Men's head-gear took a wide variety of forms in the fifteenth century. The hood, which had been popular from the twelfth century, went out of fashion after the middle of the century, although it is worn by the figure in the Victoria and Albert Museum panel mentioned above. Around 1450 turban-like hats were popular, but in the latter part of the century wide-brimmed and large-crowned hats appear more often. Both types are illustrated in the panels of the life of St Margaret at Combs, Suffolk.

In the fifteenth century the kirtle was still the normal dress for women, but is rarely shown, being hidden by the houpelande or gown. Like its male equivalent, it was long with a high or turned-over collar, very high-waisted, with a belt worn just below the breasts. The sleeves were very long, clearly shown on the figure of St Mary Magdalene at Diss, Norfolk. Around 1450 the neck was made more open in a wide V carried to the waist or below, as shown at Waterperry, Oxfordshire. Alternatively, the neckline was very low, bordered with fur, with the upper part of the gown moulded closely to the figure, shown in one of the figure panels at Long Melford, Suffolk. After 1495 the gown became looser again, with a square-cut neckline. Women's head-dress became very elaborate during this period. At first the styles were broad. Ornamental templers, elaborate fillets with two bosses of metal mesh on either side of the temples, retained the hair, and were sometimes worn to cover the ears, like headphones. A woman in the Ten Commandments window at Ludlow has such a head-dress, as do others at Hereford Cathedral and Prees, Shropshire.

The templers soon became more elaborate; around 1420 they were extended sideways from the head, giving a broad effect as shown on the figures of the wives and daughters of Richard Stowting at Stowting, Kent, and on Margaret Ros, at the bottom of the St William window at York Minster. The 'Museum' window at

Great Malvern Priory has a fragment showing a clear representation of this style. Between 1410 and 1420 the templers were swept up to form shapes like thick cow horns, and this strange head-dress was often covered by a veil. It is clearly shown at Thryberg, Yorkshire, and Holy Trinity, Goodramgate, York. Between 1420 and 1450 the points of the horns were made to curve towards each other to give a heart shape, as in an example at Thirsk, Yorkshire. Around 1440 a new style appeared. A sausage-shaped roll was bent back to a U-shape and fastened on the top of the head, the hair swept up in a net behind, with no side projections. The forehead was shaved right up to the start of the head-dress. The roll became more elongated as time went on; there is a good example of this strange fashion on the figure of Queen Elizabeth Woodville, of around 1481, at Little Malvern, Worcestershire. A high-crowned bonnet with a brim turned back and extended to hang down beside the face to the shoulders was also in fashion between 1460 and 1490. Examples can be seen in the windows at St Winnow, Cornwall, and at Windermere, Cumberland. The most remarkable fifteenth-century head-dress was the butterfly, which appeared around 1450. The hair was enclosed in a fez-like cap projecting backwards from the head. It supported a wire frame on which was hung a gauze veil, forming two filmy wings. The style, which lasted until about 1490, is well illustrated at Long Melford, Suffolk, and Waterperry, Oxfordshire. After 1485 there was a return to a small hoodlike head-dress, the face being framed with a small cap, sometimes with a veil falling behind the head down to the shoulders. An example can be seen in a small roundel of about 1500 in the vestry at Warwick, St Mary. Widows and nuns wore the veil, with a pleated wimple known as a barb.

The main innovation in male costume of the sixteenth century was the development of slashing. Slits were cut in the outer layer of cloth of jackets and so on to reveal cloth of contrasting colour below. The few representations of this fashion in stained glass include the figures of St Martin and others in the windows of St Michael le Belfrey, York. The pointed shoe was replaced by one with a broad splayed toe, clearly shown on the figure of St Martin.

Women's head-dress changed somewhat, the cap, after 1500, becoming more angular, with a point above the forehead and long straight sides hanging down below the shoulders at the front, the so-called kennel or pedimental head-dress. There are examples to be seen at Norbury, Derbyshire, and Heythrop, Shelton, and St Peter Mancroft, Norwich, in Norfolk.

Apart from the conventional dress discussed above, examples are to be found in stained glass of special clothing worn by the professions. Men of the law and medicine had their own costume, and will be dealt with later on. The members of the hierarchy of the church can be distinguished by their differing costumes, and are frequently shown in stained glass. Popes can be identified by the tiara, or triple crown; they wear richly decorated copes, or long cloaks, with the pallium, a Y-shaped ribbon with embroidered crosses, around their necks, and carry a staff with a triple cross. Archbishops, who wear the cope and pallium, carry a single cross-staff. Like bishops, they wear the mitre. In the twelfth century the mitre was flattened and rounded, with a depression in the centre and curled-over sides; it is shown thus in a French panel of the late twelfth century, at Rivenhall, Essex. In the thirteenth century the mitre was slightly taller, with a narrow brim and concave sides curving up to a sharp point, as represented at Credenhill, Herefordshire. By the next century the sides of the mitre were straighter, though the top was still pointed, and it was generally richly ornamented. A good example can be seen in the east window of Gloucester Cathedral, and others in the Lady

Chapel at Wells Cathedral. In the fifteenth century the mitre was much taller, with convex sides and a less acute point. Examples, including side views, can be seen in the bottom of the east window at York Minster. Bishops are represented with a cope, mitre and crosier or crook staff. The latter is also carried by abbots and abbesses, but they can be distinguished by their monastic habits, heavy cowled robes for the monks and wimples and veils worn by the nuns. Cardinals are shown with broad-brimmed red hats, well shown on the figure of St Jerome at Saxlingham Nethergate, Norfolk. Deacons are distinguished by the dalmatic, a long robe open at the sides rather than the front, often with an embroidered panel at the foot.

A careful study of medieval glass throughout the country will reveal all kinds of intriguing details of clothing. The 'Clothing the naked' subject at All Saints, North Street, York, shows men wearing a form of underpants of very modern appearance. In the same window a man ill in bed wears a coif, perhaps as a nightcap. The same detail is shown in a roundel of the same subject at the Old Jewry Museum, Leicester; under the bed lies the sick man's boots, with a crutch and chamber-pot. Also at Leicester, in a scene of Confirmation, the child is wrapped in the chrysom clothes, bound with diagonal bands, in which it would be kept until confirmation, and in which it would be buried if it died in infancy. Similarly swaddled babies are shown at Ashton under Lyne, Lancashire. At East Harling, Norfolk, and St Peter Mancroft, Norwich, scenes of the Visitation show St Elizabeth, pregnant with John the Baptist, in a medieval maternity garment with an open, laced-up front. From the later fifteenth century, personal jewellery is

often illustrated; necklaces in particular are shown on female donors at Long Melford, Suffolk, Morley, Derbyshire, Ashton under Lyne, Lancashire, and Waterperry, Oxfordshire. Man's final garment, the shroud, is shown in a panel of Burying the Dead, from the Acts of Mercy, at the Old Jewry Museum, Leicester.

Left : Child in a chrysom cloth, detail of a 'Confirmation' panel, about 1500 – Old Jewry Museum, Leicester; *right :* St Elizabeth, in a medieval maternity dress with a lace up front, *c.* 1480; *inset :* fragment of glass with lacing details – both East Harling, Norfolk

Armour

The evolution of armour from the twelfth to the sixteenth century can be traced in stained glass. The earliest representations, in the late-twelfth-century glass at Canterbury Cathedral, show that armour had changed little since the Norman Conquest. Knights wore suits of mail, covering them completely to the knees. Legs were protected by stockings of mail, and the head by a conical metal helmet worn over a coif of mail. Kite-shaped shields were carried for further protection. The siege of Canterbury by the Danes, and the subsequent martyrdom of St Alphege, are shown in medallion windows of around 1200 in the north choir triforium windows at Canterbury Cathedral. The mailed figures there might well have come straight from the Bayeux Tapestry, so similar are they to the Norman knights of a hundred and forty years earlier. As an alternative to the conical helmet, knights might wear larger helms which completely covered the head. They were at first domed, then, after 1200, flat-topped. At Rivenhall, Essex, there is a French panel of around 1200 showing a knight, Robert Lemaire, on horseback. Wearing a large round-topped helm, with ventilation slots, he carries a sword and 'heater'-shaped shield.

left : 'Lily Crucifixion',
1475 – Westwood,
Wiltshire; *right :* 'St Edward
the Confessor', mid-
fifteenth century – Ross on
Wye, Herefordshire

The suit of mail remained the primary protection for the knight through most of the thirteenth century. In the last decades of this period, small plates or panels were attached to the shoulders, not for protection but to provide a surface upon which heraldic devices could be displayed. This was a necessary means of identification of individuals in battle whose faces were completely concealed by the helm. These ailettes, as they were called, remained in use until around 1340. They are shown in a number of windows, including examples at Carlton Scroop, Lincolnshire, Bere Ferrers, Devon, and in the de Mauley window in the nave of York Minster. In the middle of the thirteenth century small plates of metal or hardened leather were added to the mail, usually at the knee to give further protection. The bottom part of such a device can be seen on the figure of St George, at Brinsop, Herefordshire, of around 1300, and on the rather later figures of Sir John Charlton and his sons, at Shrewsbury St Mary, Shropshire. A long linen surcoat was worn over the armour, usually embroidered with heraldic displays.

By the 1320s various bits of plate had been added to the suit of mail. Gutter-shaped plates were strapped to the front of arms and legs, and extra pieces protected arm, elbow and knee joints. The most interesting examples of armour of the early fourteenth century are in the glass at Tewkesbury Abbey, Gloucestershire. Eight figures of the family of the donor, Eleanor de Clare, are shown in armour which is different for almost every figure. Robert Fitzroy is shown in mail, with plate coverings to the legs and hands, and a rounded cap of plate on his head. Gilbert de Clare is in mail, with plate covering the legs, elbows and shoulders, and a globular plate protection covers his head. Hugh de Despencer has his legs and arms completely covered in plate, and a collar of small plates riveted together to protect his neck. Robert Fitzhamon is dressed partly in mail and partly in plate like Gilbert de Clare, but has a more pointed helmet with a mail collar attached. Richard de Clare, in full plate armour, is clearly drawn from the same cartoon as Hugh de Despencer. Gilbert de Clare I has his upper body entirely protected by plate, but with plate only at the front of his legs. Finally Gilbert de Clare II has the plate helmet and neck protection, but mail only on the arms, and the legs have part plate, part mail covering. All the figures carry swords and spears, and wear heraldic surcoats, with ailettes visible behind their shoulders. They graphically illustrate the variety of protection during the transition from mail to plate armour in the fourteenth century.

At the end of the fourteenth century the knight's outfit consisted of a mail shirt reaching to the hips, a breastplate of rather rounded shape, worn under a linen jupon, a shorter garment that had replaced the surcoat, and arms, legs and feet covered with plate protection. The helmet was pointed, and from the lower edge hung a protective collar of mail called the aventail, which reached and covered the shoulders. A fragment of glass at Farleigh Hungerford, Somerset, depicting the head of a knight, shows clearly how the mail was fastened to the helmet. Sometimes the thigh protection was covered with cloth and studded, a feature shown on the figure of Sir Jacob Berners, of around 1388, at West Horsley, Surrey, and on a figure of St George, at Castle Acre, Norfolk. At the beginning of the fifteenth century the conversion to plate armour was completed with the addition of a back plate and a plate collar, or gorget. The lower body was covered by a series of hoops of plate linked together to form a flexible skirt, and extra plates were added at the elbow, armpit and knee. The figure of St Michael, at Kingsnorth, Kent, shows this change in transition around 1400; the figure of St George at Ludlow, Shropshire, shows the plate skirt divided at the front for use on horseback. A side view of full plate armour is given by the figure of Richard Beaumont, Earl of Warwick, at Warwick, St Mary.

Around the middle of the fifteenth century a series of small plates were added to the bottom of the skirt, over each thigh, for extra protection, and are illustrated on the figure of St George at Mersham, Kent. In the second half of the century the protective plates at the arm and elbow joints became greatly enlarged and spiky, and the surface of the armour was often fluted or ribbed. The excellent figure of Sir Robert Wingfield, at East Harling, Norfolk, is finely detailed. He wears a Yorkist 'Suns and Roses' collar over a stiff collar of mail, which by about 1480 had once again replaced plate protection for the neck. Beside him is a helm with a pointed and hinged visor. The 'Gothic' armour of the continental manufacturers is shown in a Flemish panel of around 1500 at Exeter Cathedral, interesting for the variety of arms and armour it illustrates.

In the Tudor period, foot armour, which had all along had pointed toes like civilian footwear, changed to the broad-toed sabbaton. A mail skirt replaced the plate version, but sets of articulated plates were still hung in front of the thighs. An early example, of 1500, is illustrated at Prees, Shropshire, with the mail skirt but with the older, pointed toes to the foot armour. Glass of the same period at Windermere, Cumberland, shows the broader toes. Later examples are shown at Shelton, Norfolk. In some glass of continental manufacture, soldiers are shown in armour based on Roman patterns. The Resurrection window in the Lady Chapel at Lichfield Cathedral, of 1538, shows four soldiers dressed in Roman-style armour.

Tools and Furnishings

Medieval stained glass, especially that of the fifteenth century, shows many details of everyday life, and is a rich source of information regarding how people lived and worked. A few examples may serve to illustrate the variety of objects to be found shown in old glass.

Agricultural implements are often represented. The medieval spade was made of wood, with a shield-shaped blade covered at the tip with an iron rim. The iron-shod spade is the first tool to be represented in the surviving glass; one is being used by Adam in a figure panel of around 1190 in the west window of Canterbury Cathedral. The spade remained virtually unchanged throughout the Middle Ages; an almost identical example is shown in the foreground of a burial scene of about 1500 at the Old Jewry Museum, Leicester. A spade with an all-metal blade is illustrated in a Flemish panel of the Life of St Bernard, of similar date, at Shrewsbury, St Mary. The theme of 'The Labours of the Months' was a popular one for domestic glazing, and a number of examples from such series have found their way into churches. The normal form is a roundel, often in enamel and silver stain only, showing the countryman's activities in each month of the year. The choice of subject for the months can vary, but the following are typical: January, drinking at home or spinning; February, sitting by the fire; March, pruning or sowing; April, planting or bird-scaring; May, hunting; June, mowing; July, weeding or haymaking; August, reaping or fruit-picking; September, threshing, hunting or grape-picking; October, beating oak-trees for acorns or sowing; November, pig-killing; December, wood-chopping or feasting.

There are no complete sets of Labours in a church, but individual examples can be found at a number of places, including Dewsbury, Yorkshire, Checkley, Staffordshire, Lanteglos by Fowey, Cornwall, Lincoln Cathedral and the Victoria and Albert Museum, London. Among other implements, they show pruning-

Labours of the Months; *above, left :* March, pruning *below, left :* July, mowing; *above right :* October, sowing; *below, right :* November, killing a pig – Victoria and Albert Museum, London

[82]

knives, poleaxes and scythes. The last tool is the emblem of St Sidwell, who is
shown with one in the east window of Exeter Cathedral. At St Neot, Cornwall,
a plough is shown, pulled by deer, and at Glasgow Art Gallery a German panel
gives a detailed illustration of a plough at work. Seed-sowing is shown in two
panels of glass of about 1200 in the north choir aisle windows at Canterbury
Cathedral. They show two methods of carrying the seed; one in a cloth tied by one
end to the shoulder and held at the other, and the other in a basket slung round the

neck, the method used in an early-fifteenth-century representation at the Victoria and Albert Museum.

The tools of various trades and crafts may be shown as the emblems of saints or in use in narrative panels. A smithy is shown in a Flemish panel of around 1500 at Exeter Cathedral, and smith's tongs are held by St Apollonia at North Cadbury, Somerset, and St Agatha, at South Creake, Norfolk. Carpenter's tools are shown at Twycross, Leicestershire, where in a French panel of about 1243 a man uses pincers and a claw hammer to remove the nail from Christ's feet. A panel at Morley, Derbyshire, shows carpenters making the Cross, using a saw, set-square, adze and auger. The saw is an emblem of the Apostle Simon, and he is shown with one in the glass at Ludlow, Shropshire. St Thomas Didymus, who was a carpenter, is usually shown with a set-square, as he is in the east window of Selby Abbey, Yorkshire. At Canterbury Cathedral a carpenter is shown shaping a wooden beam, laid on trestles, with an axe, which has slipped and injured his leg. Dividers are used by God during the Creation, as shown in the narrative windows at St Neot, Cornwall, and Great Malvern Priory. Bellfounding is shown in a fourteenth-century window at York Minster. Although the glass is badly damaged it is possible to make out the casting and tuning operations. At Fairford, Gloucestershire, glassmaker's furnaces and grinding mills are among the devices used to torture souls in hell. Building tools and methods, including a plumbline, mason's tools and mortar mixing, are shown in a sixteenth-century panel at Southend-on-Sea.

Wheeled vehicles are not often shown in stained glass, although at Fairford, devils use handcarts and wheelbarrows to carry souls off to hell, and a large, four-wheeled wagon is used for the same purpose in a Doom window at Ticehurst, Sussex. Ships and boats, on the other hand, are quite often shown. Noah's Ark is represented in many places, including thirteenth-century examples at Canterbury and Lincoln Cathedrals, and detailed representations of the fifteenth century at Great Malvern Priory and St Neot, Cornwall. Other ships can be seen at Canterbury Cathedral (where one has a dragon-head prow like the Viking ships), Ludlow, Shropshire; Greystoke, Cumberland; and Orchardleigh, Somerset, where it is carried by St Jude as his emblem.

Domestic utensils and furnishings are often illustrated. Beds are shown in a number of the early-thirteenth-century panels in the Trinity Chapel at Canterbury Cathedral, where they are shown as low, with short pillars at each corner. More detailed representations are given in Nativity scenes and such subjects as Visiting the Sick or Extreme Unction, especially in the fifteenth century. At All Saints, North Street, in the Acts of Mercy window, a bed is shown with a flower-patterned bedspread and a pillow covered by an open-ended pillowcase. Several beds are shown in the glass preserved at the Old Jewry Museum, Leicester. They range from a simple, divan-like bed with a long bolster pillow, through one with a part canopy or tester, with a short fringed hanging, to a full four-poster, with hanging curtains and fringed edge to the canopy. This scene also includes a cradle, suspended in a standing frame and rocked by two angels. A more elaborate bed, with a tester and fringed drapes, is shown in a sixteenth-century Flemish panel at Southend-on-Sea, Essex. Almost all scenes of the Nativity, sick-beds and death-beds include a small, horseshoe-shaped armchair. It is almost certainly a close stool, or night commode, a necessary item for the sick-room, especially in the days before the introduction of the indoor watercloset. It is shown in windows at St Peter Mancroft, Norwich; East Harling, Norfolk; All Saints, North Street,

York; St Neot, Cornwall; Crudwell, Wiltshire; Doddiscombleigh, Devon; Cartmel Fell, Lancashire; and the Old Jewry Museum, Leicester.

In a scene of the birth of the Virgin, at Gresford, Denbighshire, a servant cooks food in a shallow saucepan or frying-pan over a fire held in a large, shallow, circular bowl just by the bed. Another cooking utensil often seen is the grid-iron, the emblem of St Lawrence, and carried by him in glass at Nettlestead, Kent; Thaxted, Essex; Weston Underwood, Buckinghamshire; and many other places. A grid-iron is shown in use, grilling fish, in a Life of St Neot window, at St Neot, Cornwall. The Feast at Cana and Last Supper subjects usually display a variety of tableware, drinking vessels and food. Medieval loaves were tall, with domed, crusty tops and flattened sides. They are shown in the Acts of Mercy window at All Saints, North Street, York, at Combs, Suffolk, and Great Malvern Priory, in the Last Supper panels.

Lamps and lanterns are occasionally illustrated in old glass. The Betrayal panel at East Harling, Norfolk, shows several enclosed candle lanterns and a portable brazier or cresset on a pole. The Wise and Foolish Virgins of the parable carry oil-lamps, illustrated at Melbury Bubb, Dorset. Medieval coinage had a representation of the monarch on one face and a cross on the other, with a pattern of dots between the arms of the cross. It is this face that is generally shown when coins are represented, as they are in the Visiting the Sick subject at All Saints, North Street, York. Writing instruments may be shown; at Saxlingham Nethergate, Norfolk, St Jerome and St Ambrose are shown seated at writing-desks, one with an inkhorn and the other with an ink-bottle. At Gresford, Denbighshire, a monk is shown wearing an ink-bottle and pencase on his belt. At Stratton Strawless, Norfolk, St Luke is shown with a brush and long palette. A man is shown wearing spectacles in a fragment of glass in the Corpus Christi window at All Saints, North Street, York, and the man circumcising Christ in the window at King's College Chapel wears them also. Even children's toys sometimes appear in glass. The children of St Mary Cleophas, in a window at Thornhill, Yorkshire, play with a peg-top and whip, and something that looks a little like the front of a modern scooter, but which cannot be positively identified. The same family are shown at Holy Trinity, Goodramgate, York, where the young St Jude plays with a toy boat. At Hessett, Suffolk, in a fifteenth-century panel, a boy holds a bat very like a hockey-stick, and in the north choir aisle window at Canterbury Cathedral, of around 1200, a boy is shown with a similar bat, and a ball, in the Six Ages of Man panel.

Musical instruments
A great variety of musical instruments are represented in medieval glass. They are normally played by angels, but some, like the harp of King David or the organ of St Cecilia, are identificatory emblems. The earliest representation of a musical instrument in glass is that of the harp played by King David in a panel of about 1190 in the south transept window of Canterbury Cathedral. There are a few instruments illustrated in glass of the next two centuries, but it is not until the fifteenth century that they become at all common. In this period musical angels were used to fill tracery lights, the most spectacular examples being at Warwick, St Mary. The ensemble playing of musicians had become common only in Europe at the time of the last Crusades, at the beginning of the thirteenth century, and then mainly for military purposes. At the end of the fourteenth century bands of wind instruments were used to accompany dancing, and it may be that this

new, peaceful use of the band prompted its adoption as a symbol of joyous praise. The four main divisions of the modern orchestra – strings, woodwind, brass and percussion – were represented in medieval times.

The most common stringed instrument played by angels was not, as might be expected, the harp, but the lute. There are more representations of this instrument than any other in medieval glass. Brought to Europe during the Crusades of the thirteenth century, it was generally played with a quill plectrum, although it could also be plucked directly with the fingers. There are many examples, among them those at Martham, Cawston and Emneth in Norfolk; Newark, Nottinghamshire; Orchardleigh, Somerset; and the Victoria and Albert Museum. All show the lute played with a quill plectrum. The cittern was related to the lute, but had metal strings and a shape more like that of a guitar. It is probably the instrument played by an angel in fourteenth-century glass in the north transept of Lincoln Cathedral.

The harp was a very ancient instrument, which may have been brought to Europe from the east by Irish travellers. It was certainly in widespread use in Ireland and England by the eleventh century. Most Jesse Tree windows include a figure of King David with his harp. Typical examples of angels playing this instrument occur at Barkway, Hertfordshire (where the harp has a grotesque head for decoration); Great Chart, Kent; Emneth, Martham and Mulbarton, Norfolk; Orchardleigh, Somerset; and the Victoria and Albert Museum. The psaltery was another plucked string instrument, in appearance rather like a zither, but without frets, the strings being open. It was usually played lying across the lap or held on the knees, but might be held vertically against the chest. There are good illustrations at Cawston, Burnham Deepdale (of the fourteenth century) and Shelton, Norfolk; Thornhill and York Minster (in the north choir aisle east window), Yorkshire; and Orchardleigh, Somerset.

The second group of stringed instruments were played with a bow, a development, it is believed, of the thirteenth century. In the Middle Ages the bow was deeply curved, like the weapon of the same name. The rebec, an instrument of Byzantine origin, was one of the most popular. It had a deeply curved body like the lute, tapering gradually to the neck. It is shown at Warwick, St Mary, Orchardleigh, and Great Malvern Priory (north transept north window) and elsewhere. The rebec was an example of a group of bowed instruments given the generic name of fiddles. Another form, which was to evolve into the modern violin, had a flattened body of more rectangular outline than the rebec, with a more abrupt transition from body to neck. A six-stringed example of the fourteenth century is in the north transept glass at Lincoln Cathedral; a later, less detailed instance is in the west window of Attleborough church, Norfolk. Fifteenth-century examples are at Saxlingham Nethergate and St Peter Hungate, Norwich, in Norfolk; Warwick, St Mary and the Victoria and Albert Museum. In the glass at Warwick there are strange instruments played with bows. They are roughly rectangular, with two holes through the body, on either side of the strings, through which the fingers pass, from below. They are probably bowed lyres, like the Welsh crwth. The tromba marina was another odd stringed instrument, very popular in medieval times. It had a long, straight-sided, tapering shape, with a single string played with a bow, and is shown in the Warwick glass.

The third type of stringed instrument was played by striking the strings instead of bowing or plucking. The dulcimer was similar in appearance to the psaltery, but was played by striking the strings with hammers. An example is shown in a window at Stratton Strawless, Norfolk. Some instruments were played by a keyboard mechanism. The clavichord, first recorded in the early fifteenth century, is shown in its simplest form at Warwick. A roughly rectangular shallow box has strings running along its length. On one of the longer sides are a series of keys which operate a simple striking mechanism. An early virginal is also shown at Warwick. It has the shape of a small grand piano, with strings of different length, plucked by a keyboard-operated mechanism, like the harpsichord into which it evolved. The hurdy-gurdy, or organistrum, was played by operating keys, but had more of the characteristics of a bowed instrument. When a handle at one end was turned, a rosin-covered wheel rotated against the strings, vibrating them. The keys, when pressed, varied the pitch of the note by stopping the strings at suitable points. One is shown in the north transept window at Great Malvern Priory.

The earliest wind instruments shown in medieval glass are the long and slightly curved trumpet-like instruments played by angels in the scenes of the Last Judgement in the early-thirteenth-century rose window at Lincoln Cathedral. Although they may be meant to represent brass trumpets, they are more likely to be cornetts, which although played like brass instruments were made of wood. They were reedless, with bell-shaped mouthpieces and fingerholes to vary the pitch of the notes. The pipe appears in several forms; the simplest type had only two holes on the top and one, for the thumb, below. An example is in the Warwick glass. The flageolet had four fingerholes above and two below, and is clearly shown at Warham St Mary, Norfolk, while others are shown at Warwick. The recorder, with seven holes above and one below, first appeared in the fifteenth century and is shown at Great Malvern Priory and at Fairford, Gloucestershire.

Wind instruments employing a mouthpiece with a vibrating reed to give a more complex sound are of very ancient origin. One simple medieval form was the horn-pipe, a reed pipe fitted with a horn, usually from a cow, at the end. Double and single hornpipes are shown at Warwick, and the double form is clearly shown, played by a shepherd at the Nativity, at East Harling, Norfolk. The bagpipe is a related instrument, being a simple reed pipe supplied by air from an inflated bag rather than directly. The medieval form was rather less elaborate than the modern Scots version; it is shown at Warwick, Shelton, Norfolk, Norwich Cathedral (an ornate version, in the north choir aisle window), Fairford, Gloucestershire, and Orchardleigh, Somerset. The shawm, forerunner of the oboe, was usually played held horizontally, like a trumpet to give maximum sound dispersion. One of the clearest representations is in a Nativity scene at Newark House, Leicester. The organ is another wind instrument of great antiquity; a pneumatic type was almost certainly in use in Byzantium in the fifth century. Early examples, like the great organ built at Winchester in the tenth century, were played by cumbersome slides. Major improvements, notably in the use of a simple lever keyboard, were made after the year 1000. Simple organs are shown in glass of around 1400 at Boughton Aluph, Kent. More usually represented are the portative organs, made to be carried in processions. Good examples can be seen at Warwick, Shelton, Norfolk, and Charlinch and Farleigh Hungerford in Somerset. In the latter two cases it is carried by St Cecilia, one of whose emblems it is.

The two principal brass instruments of medieval times were the trumpet and sackbut, or trombone. The latter may be one of the instruments played by angels in the north transept window at Great Malvern Priory, but the details are obscured by a repair. The trumpet, in its original form, was long and straight, like the posthorn. It is clearly shown held by the Archangel Gabriel in fifteenth-century glass at Long Melford, Suffolk. In the fifteenth century a folded form, like a squashed letter S, had evolved, and may be the instrument played by a sad-looking angel at Great Chart, Kent, although it appears to have a mouthpiece

 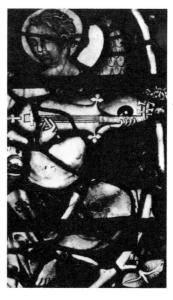  

The celestial orchestra;
above, left to right : Lute –
Cawston, Norfolk; Cittern –
Lincoln Cathedral; Fiddle –
Saxlingham Nethergate,
Norfolk; Bowed lyres or
crwths – Warwick, St Mary
below, left to right : Virginal
Warwick, St Mary; Psaltery
– Cawston, Norfolk; Harp –
Barkway, Hertfordshire;
Clavichord – Warwick, St
Mary

ove, left to right : Dulcimer
Stratton Strawless,
orfolk; Kettledrums –
rkway, Hertfordshire;
usical Bowls – Warwick,
Mary; Bagpipes – St
ter Hungate, Norwich;
ornpipes – East Harling,
orfolk; *below, left to right :*
ageolet and tabor –
arham St Mary, Norfolk;
rumpet – Wells Cathedral,
merset; Portative organ –
arwick, St Mary; Choral
gels – Warwick, St Mary

more like a reed instrument. A trumpet with an open S-shape is played by an angel in glass at Leigh on Mendip, Somerset.

The fourth group of instruments are of the percussion type. The tabor, a small snare drum usually played in accompaniment to pipes, is shown at Warham St Mary, Norfolk, Warwick and Great Malvern Priory. A small pair of kettledrums is played by an angel in a window at Barkway, Hertfordshire. The tambourine, a very ancient percussion instrument, is shown in the Warwick glass, as is the triangle, also shown at Gresford, Denbighshire. At Warwick an angel with a small hammer plays a series of bowls of graduated sizes.

Singing angels are shown with books or sheets of music in a few places, as at Shelton, Norfolk, and Fairford, Gloucestershire. At Warwick the windows of instrument-playing angels alternate with others with angels carrying the words and music of the antiphon 'Gaudeamus', while seraphim in the east window sing the plain-song 'Ave Regina' from scrolls of music.

Medicine

We cannot learn much of the state of medical knowledge in the middle ages directly, from stained glass, but indirectly there is much to be discovered, especially from the 'miracle' windows at Canterbury and York. The martyrdom of Thomas à Becket in 1170 was soon followed by accounts of miracles worked at his tomb in Ernulf's crypt, to which the public had been given access from April 1171. Over the next fifty years increasing numbers of pilgrims, many seriously ill or crippled when they arrived, went away cured. Around and over the tomb a masonry structure had been built, with oval apertures through which the visitor could kiss the tomb or pass a diseased limb for healing. The tomb is shown many times in the windows of the Trinity Chapel of Canterbury Cathedral, painted around 1220.

For the benefit of those unable to travel, pilgrims could purchase specimens of the dead saint's blood, heavily diluted with water. After the martyrdom, the monks had collected the spilt blood, and preserved Becket's bloodstained clothes. When these relics proved efficacious, and the demand grew too great, the blood was mixed with water, since a minute speck of blood was thought to be effective in treating a large quantity of water, which then acquired miraculous properties. Several panels in the Trinity Chapel show the ritual of mixing the blood, from a vial, in a large basin, with a long spoon. Since some of Becket's blood had run into a nearby well, the water from this was considered holy, and gave an inexhaustible supply of healing fluid. Pilgrims could purchase small lead flasks of holy water, and these are often shown in the windows.

Later, Becket's remains were moved to the newly built Trinity Chapel, to a golden, jewelled shrine, which is represented in several of the panels. These windows are a catalogue of the miracles performed at the tomb and shrine, and the illnesses they represent are clearly those for which no treatment was known or effective. There is a distinctly commercial air about the way in which great emphasis was placed on the necessity of making generous donations, usually of gold wire, to the cathedral, if the treatment were to be successful. Examples of one or two of the case histories illustrated will indicate some of the medical problems of the Middle Ages.

A lad, Richard Sunieve of Edgeworth, was employed as a horse-drover by Richard Fitzhenry. Sleeping one day while his horses grazed, he contracted leprosy, and woke to find himself infected. In the glass, he is shown in bed, while his mother, her face covered against infection, brings him food on a tray. Soon he was shunned by almost everyone, even his mother being reluctant to go near him. He was cured by visiting the tomb, praying to St Thomas and drinking some holy water. In another panel he is healed, showing his face to his master; the inscription reads, 'His flesh becomes as before, his complexion and strength and carriage are the same'. Finally he is shown making the obligatory donation.

The constant threat of plague is illustrated in another series of panels. Plague struck the house of Sir Jordan Fitzeisulf, a friend of Becket's, and killed the nurse Britonis, whose bier is shown carried by four men. Next, Sir Jordan's ten-year-old son contracted the disease and died. As his body lay on the bier, pilgrims arrived from Canterbury with holy water. Some was poured into the dead child's mouth, while a holy vow was made to present money to the Saint if the prayers were answered. The boy was restored to life, but the family did not honour their promise. A leper called Gimp was visited in a dream by St Thomas, who gave a warning that the vow must be kept. This warning ignored, an elder son was struck down with the plague and the whole family was made ill, until Sir Jordan made good his promise of an offering.

Mental as well as physical illnesses were cured. Henry of Fordwich, who was mad, is shown being dragged to the tomb with his hands bound behind him and being beaten with birches by two custodians. He is cured, and in another panel gives thanks, his bonds discarded. In another panel, a homicidal maniac, Matilda of Cologne, is brought to the tomb, also, like Henry, beaten by her keepers. 'She alternates her bearing, now sane and [now] troublesome'. She collapses at the tomb, and rises cured. In another story Stephen of Hoylake is cured of nightmares, symbolised by demons around his bed.

Among the many other afflictions cured at the shrine are a child's hernia (cured by application of a rag from St Thomas's shirt), wounds by axe and arrow, death by drowning, blindness, lameness, deafness, dropsy, quartan fever, 'tormenting of the bowels', epilepsy, palsy and swollen feet. The windows are like a vast medieval advertisement, emphasising the virtues of the 'product', which could cure all known ills, for a price.

As a result of these miracles, Canterbury rapidly became the major centre for pilgrimage in Britain. This clearly upset the authorities at York, who, not to be outdone, promoted the virtues of their own celebrity, St William of York. He was a treasurer of the Minster in the twelfth century, who was enthroned as archbishop in 1154, only to die weeks later. After representations to the Pope, he was canonised in 1226, and stories began to spread of miracles taking place at his tomb. Around 1283 his remains were removed to a special shrine behind the high altar. This shrine is shown many times in the great window set in about 1422 to commemorate the life and miracles of St William. In the two hundred years separating the Canterbury and York windows, little had changed in the incidence of disease. Among the conditions cured at the shrine, according to the stories in the window, were paralysis, dropsy, deformity, lost eyes, blindness, poisoning, deafness, drowning and leprosy. York did not have the advantage of a holy water well, but a sufferer unfit to travel to York could still find relief. The St William window includes panels showing the measurement of a diseased leg in the preparation of a wax model. In another panel, the model is presented at the shrine, on which are hung other models of a heart, a woman's head and an arm. Thus, the presentation of a proxy limb or organ was deemed to be almost as good as a personal visit. In another panel a man eats mortar taken from the tomb, in the hope of a cure.

There are several saints who have connections with medicine and who may be portrayed in stained glass. St Roch was a fourteenth-century Frenchman who gave up his wealth to travel to Rome to enter a religious life. On the way, passing through a town struck by the plague, he stayed to tend for and cure the sick, and decided to make this his life's work. He travelled the country to wherever the plague was found, until he finally contracted the disease himself. He went into the country to die, but recovered, helped by his dog, who brought him food every day. His changed appearance caused him to be locked away as a spy, and he died in prison, some years later. At Littleham, Devon, he is represented in pilgrim's clothing, with a staff, his robe raised to show a plague spot on his thigh. At Barkway, Hertfordshire, an angel is applying ointment to the spot from a small dish. He was the patron saint of the sick. especially those ill with the plague.

Saints Cosmo and Damian were two brothers, physicians who spent their lives healing the sick, until their martyrdom as Christians in the fourth century. They were patron saints of the medical profession, but do not appear to be represented in surviving glass. At Minster Lovell, Oxfordshire, there is the figure of a doctor of the fifteenth century. He wears the beret-like cap and fur-trimmed robe of an academic, and carries a sword in one hand and a urine flask held up for inspection in the other. Diagnosis of disease by inspecting the colour and clarity of urine was a usual medieval practice. The figure is almost certainly that of the physician St Pantaleon, of Nicodema, martyred by beheading in the fourth century. A urine inspection is shown in the Trinity Chapel glass at Canterbury Cathedral, where two physicians consult over a leprous monk, Elias of Reading. One inspects the specimen, while the other examines the patient.

The archangel Raphael appears twice in the fifteenth-century glass at Bolton Percy, Yorkshire, anointing the eyes of an elderly blind man with salve applied by a feather. This subject is based upon the apochryphal story of Tobias and the Angel. Raphael appears to Tobias, who has caught a large fish, telling him that 'the gall . . . is good to anoint a man that hath whiteness in his eyes, and he shall be healed.' With the fish's gall, Tobias was able to cure his father's blindness. For this reason, St Raphael was invoked against eye disease and was the patron saint of apothecaries.

Unless they were of rich families, those who lost the use of their limbs through crippling disease had to become beggars. Two crippled beggars are seen in the Acts of Mercy window at All Saints, North Street. A man with a crutch holds out his bowl to the benefactor, while beside him a man kneels on the ground waiting his turn. His knees are covered with a studded protection, and he has two hand-crutches, like small, three-legged stools, to protect his hands when propelling himself along the rough roads. Similar hand-crutches are shown in the St William window in York Minster.

The law
The legal profession is represented in medieval glass from time to time. In the early glass of Trinity Chapel, at Canterbury Cathedral, of around 1220, a magistrate or judge is shown presiding over a trial by combat. He is distinguished only by a staff of office; his dress is like that of others in the glass. By the fifteenth century the officers of the law had been designated in distinct classes, each with its own features of dress. Legal costume of this period falls between that of ecclesiastic and academic dress. Long, fur-trimmed robes were worn over a form of cassock, and often a coif, tied under the chin, although the latter is sometimes shown on figures of people not connected with the law, especially in York glass. There are fine examples at Long Melford, Suffolk. Two figures, drawn from the same cartoon, are of John Haugh, Judge of Assize and Sergeant at Law, and Richard Pigot,

Sergeant at Law. Both are in fur-trimmed purple robes with fur collars. A third figure, of Sir William Howard, Chief Justice of Common Pleas, wears a more sumptuous red robe, with richer fur trimming. All three wear the coif.

The representation of trial by combat, mentioned above, illustrates a judicial process of great antiquity which, by the tenth century, had come to be applied to even quite minor cases. The outcome of the battle between litigants, or their representatives, decided the case on the assumption that divine help would ensure that right would triumph. In the Canterbury glass, two men fight before a judge with shields and cudgels. In a second panel one man has picked the other, smaller man off the ground, rather as a wrestler makes a cross-buttock throw. The weaker man invokes St Thomas's help. The panel showing the outcome is missing, but the innocent party undoubtedly won. Ordeal by fire was another ancient method of establishing innocence. It was assumed that if in the right, God would protect one from harm when the hand was held in the flames or touched by a red-hot iron. In the St William window at York Minster, a woman undergoes the ordeal and escapes unharmed, by invoking St William's help. In another panel she shows her uninjured hand to the Justice.

The punishments for even trivial offences could be severe. In the Canterbury glass is the story of Eilward of Westoning, who stole a whetstone and ditching gloves from a neighbour, Fulk, to settle a debt. He is shown, in one medallion, with his hands tied behind his back and bound with rope, before a magistrate. He was given a sentence, harsh even by the standards of the day, following an ordeal by water. His eyes were cut out, and he was castrated. A second medallion shows the sentence being carried out. After invoking St Thomas, he was miraculously restored. Instruments of punishment are shown in Passion windows, and occur among the Passion symbols. Scourges, birches and cat-o'-nine-tails whips and scourging posts are represented at Westwood, Wiltshire, St Kew, Cornwall, and Martham, Norfolk. The stocks are illustrated in detail in the Visiting the Prisoners panel at All Saints, North Street, York. Three men, with their feet firmly fixed in the stocks, are fettered by their necks, hands and feet. While the benefactor brings them food, drink and money, a constable with a baton looks on, perhaps a trifle disapprovingly. Fetters and chains are the emblems of St Leonard, and thus appear in representations of this saint, who appears for some reason to be especially popular in the west country, appearing in glass at St Weonard, St Neot and St Winnow in Cornwall, Farleigh Hungerford, Somerset, and Loders, Devon. In the east window tracery of Beverley Minster, Yorkshire, he is shown holding a small pillory, while in a larger light below he has the more usual chains. Prisons are shown in some places, as at Greystoke, Cumberland, where St Matthew preaches from a cell window, or at Combs, where St Margaret is chained and cast into a dungeon. At St Patrick's Chapel, Glastonbury, Somerset, is a fragment of glass showing prisoners looking from a cell window, part of a Visiting the Prisoners subject. A sixteenth-century panel at St Michael le Belfrey, York, shows the arrest of a young man, manacled outside a prison. The commission of a crime is shown at Ludlow, where in the Ten Commandments window a thief cuts the purse from a rich man's belt.

6

WHERE TO SEE MEDIEVAL GLASS

THE county lists that follow include most of the places where significant remains may be found. Many other churches, however, possess fragments of old glass. Indeed, there are few churches of medieval foundation in which careful searching will not reveal pieces of glass of ancient origin. The author has inspected most of the places listed; information about others has been extracted from a variety of sources, notably *The Buildings of England*, written and edited by Sir Nicholas Pevsner for Penguin Books. The lists are arranged under the county divisions prevailing before the changes in local administration. Since all the earlier literature on stained glass, maps and gazeteers is arranged thus, it was thought desirable to retain the older demarcations in the present work.

Where possible, the approximate location of the glass within the church is given. The medieval church was laid out on an east-to-west line, with the altar at the east. The visitor may thus easily be orientated. For definitions of the architectural terms used in the lists, the reader is referred to the glossary. Remember that, due to restoration, insertion or new windows and, rarely, destruction, the location of some glass may have altered since this information was compiled and have to be sought elsewhere in the church. In any case, all windows in the church being visited should be inspected, as other fragments not mentioned in the lists may well deserve attention. For the most part only the principal and reasonably complete figures and panels have been noted. In the case of the cathedrals, such as Canterbury and York, or the larger churches, such as Great Malvern Priory, only an outline is given of the content of windows. For more detailed information the works listed in the bibliography are recommended.

BEDFORDSHIRE

Barton-in-the-Clay 14th-century figure of St James, north aisle window.

Bolnhurst 15th-century Virgin and Child, north-east window.

Cockayne Hatby Early-14th-century figures of SS Oswald, Edward, Ethelbald and Dunstan, north aisle east window.

Colmworth 15th-century archangel, chancel north-west window.

Dean 15th-century figure of a priest, south aisle west window.

Edworth 14th-century grisaille glass and figure of St Edmund, chancel south window; 15th-century figure of St James, south clerestory window.

Luton, St Mary 15th-century figures of the Virgin and angels, Wenlock Chapel east window; 15th-century donors, room over south porch.

Marston Mortayne 16th-century glass, east window, north side.

Odell 15th-century roundels of Evangelist's symbols, etc., chancel south window; 15th-century seraphim, south aisle east window.

Old Warden Early-14th-century figure of abbot, much restored, north window.

Pavenham 15th-century roundel.

Wilden 15th-century figure of St James, east window.

BERKSHIRE

Aldermaston 13th-century panels of the Annunciation and the Coronation of the Virgin, chancel north window.

Binfield 15th-century figures, south-east window.

Childrey 15th-century panels of the Crucifixion, Ascension, Nativity, Assumption, Annunciation, with tracery angels, north transept north window.

Compton Beauchamp 14th-century panels of Annunciation and Crucifixion, east window tracery and east window, north transept.

East Hagbourne 14th-century panels of the Nativity and Purification.

East Shefford Early-16th-century panel of the Annunciation.

Goosey 15th-century figure, nave window.

Lambourn 16th-century figure of St John Evangelist.

Letcombe Regis 16th-century figure of Christ in Majesty and shields, east window.

North Moreton c.1300, fifteen panels of subjects from lives of Christ, Virgin, SS Nicholas, Peter and Paul, Stapleton Chantry chapel; 14th-century panel of Crucifixion, quarries, etc.

Radley 16th-century heraldic glass.

Shottesbrooke 14th-century figures.

Stanford-in-the-Vale 15th-century angels, east window.

Stratfield Mortimer 14th-century figure of William of Wykeham, behind the organ.

Wantage 14th-century figures, south transept; 15th-century glass in chancel.

Warfield Early-14th-century censing angels, east window.

Windsor, St George's Chapel c.1500, sixty-five figures, restored in the 18th century, west window.

Wytham 15th-century figures and panels, including St George and the Virgin, nave windows.

BUCKINGHAMSHIRE

Aston Sandford c.1280, figure of Christ enthroned.

Chenies Early-16th-century figure.

Chetwode 13th-century grisaille roundels; c.1250, figure of St John Baptist; c.1325, figures of St Nicholas and archbishop.

Drayton Beauchamp c.1300, heraldic glass, chancel south; 15th-century figures of Apostles (restored), east window.

Haddenham 15th-century figures of SS John Baptist, Bartholomew, Matthew and Paul, and angels; north chapel east window.

Hillesden 15th-century figures of Pope and bishop, east window; early-16th-century panels of the miracles of St Nicholas, east window, south aisle.

Hitcham c.1340, figure of Christ in Majesty, angels, Evangelists in chancel windows.

Langley Marsh 15th-century figure and heraldic glass.

Linslade St Mary 15th-century royal figures, west window.

Lee (old church) 13th-century figures of saints, east window.

Lower Winchendon 15th-century figure of St Peter, nave south-west window; 16th-century Flemish panel.

Ludgershall 14th-century figure of Christ, east window, north aisle.

Maids Morton 15th-century tracery figures.

Monks Risborough 15th-century figures of Virgin and Child and saint, south aisle south-east window.

Radclive 14th-century figures of Virgin and Apostle.

Stoke Hammond 15th-century figures of four prophets and two bishops in tracery.

Weston Turville 15th-century figures of Virgin and Child, east window.

Weston Underwood c.1400, figures of SS Peter, John Baptist, John Evangelist, Laurence and Paul, a bishop, with Christ in Majesty and angels in the tracery, east window, restored.

Wing 14th-century shield, with figures of Christ and the Virgin, St Catherine's Chapel east window.

CAMBRIDGESHIRE

Cambridge, Christ's College Chapel c.1475, large figures; c.1505, small figures in north windows.

Cambridge, Corpus Christi College Chapel 16th-century French panels in north and south windows.

Cambridge, King's College Chapel 1515–31, twenty-five large windows with their original glass. Several of the north and south chapels have glass of the 15th and 16th centuries.

Haslingfield c.1370, two figures, in vestry.

Landbeach 16th-century figures of first Duke and Duchess of Somerset, east window.

Leverington 15th-century Jesse Tree – thirteen figures original, seventeen restored, the rest 19th-century additions, east window; 15th-century figures of Pieta and donors, south chapel east window.

Madingley 15th-century figure of the Virgin; 16th-century panel of the Crucifixion, chancel south window.

Meldreth Early-14th-century figures of St John Baptist and monk, in tracery.

Trumpington c.1300, figures of SS Peter and Paul, chancel north window.

Wisbech St Mary c.1535, foreign panels.

CHESHIRE

Astbury c.1500, figures of St Anne and the Virgin, north aisle window.

Birtles Early-16th-century Netherlandish figures of the Virgin, St John Evangelist and angel, east window.

Bramhall Hall Chapel Early-16th-century panel of Crucifixion, east window.

Chester, St Mary's on the Hill 16th-century Passion shields, south chapel east window.

Disley c.1535, eleven panels of Passion scenes and saints, east window; six panels of Passion and Creation scenes, east window above chancel arch. German or Dutch glass.

Grappenhall c.1334, figures of SS Philip, Mary Magdalene, Peter, Thomas, James Great, John Baptist and Bartholomew, south chapel south-east window.

Mobberley 14th-century figures of donors, south aisle east window; 15th-century heraldic glass, chancel south window.

Above, left: 'St Michael', c. 1325 – north choir aisle, Wells Cathedral, Somerset; *right:* 'King Ozias', from a Jesse Tree, first half of the fourteenth century – Madley, Herefordshire; *below, left:* 'Crucifixion', c. 1330 – Mamble, Worcestershire; *right:* 'St Anne and the Virgin', mid-fourteenth century – Marsh Baldon, Oxfordshire

Above: 'Giving Shelter to the Pilgrim'; *below:* 'Visit the Prisoners', both from Acts of Mercy window, mid-fifteenth century – A Saints, North Street, York

Over Peover 1515, figure of John Mainwaring.

Plemstall 15th-century figures of donors Thomas and Margaret Smyth and children, south window.

Pott Shrigley Late-15th-century figure of St John Baptist, very restored, east window.

Shotwick 14th-century quatrefoil of the Annunciation, north aisle east window tracery.

Tattenhall Early-14th-century figures of SS Stephen and Alban, chancel south window.

CORNWALL

Golant 15th-century figures of SS Anthony and Sampson.

Laneast 15th-century panels of Crucifixion and St Gulval, east window; 15th-century Passion shields, south aisle window.

Lanteglos by Camelford 15th-century figures of the Virgin and SS Peter, Andrew, James Great, Philip and Bartholomew, south aisle window tracery.

Lanteglos by Fowey Late-15th-century panels of the Annunciation and Coronation of the Virgin, south aisle east window. January, of Labours of the Months, north aisle.

Mullion 15th-century figures of the Virgin and Child, east window.

St Kew 1469, twelve panels of life and Passion of Christ, north aisle east window; 15th-century Jesse Tree, south aisle east window; Evangelist's symbols, north aisle.

St Neot 15th century, twelve panels of life of St George, north aisle west window; *c*.1530, twelve panels of life of St Neot, nave north-west window; *c*.1530, figures of SS John, Gregory, Leonard and Andrew with donors, north aisle, second window from east; 1523, figures of SS Mabena and Menbred of Cardingham, with Pieta, Christ and donors, north aisle, third window from east; 1529, figures of SS Patrick, Clare, Manacus of Lanreath with God and donors, north aisle, fourth window from east; 16th-century figures of SS John and Stephen with Virgin and Child and Crucifixion and donors, south aisle, third window from east; 16th-century figures of SS Matthew, Mark, Luke and John, south aisle, fourth window from east; *c*.1530, figures of Saints Callawy, Germain, John and Stephen, with donors, south aisle, fifth window from east; 16th-century figures of SS Peter, Paul and James Great and Christ and Annunciation, south aisle, sixth window from east; 16th-century figures of SS Christopher, Neot, Leonard and Catherine with donors, south aisle, second window from east; 15th century, fifteen panels of the Creation, with Nine Orders of Angels in tracery, south aisle east window; *c*.1500, eight panels of the story of Noah, very restored, south aisle, first window from east.

St Winnow Late-15th-century figures of SS George, Christopher, Michael, Winnow, Mary Magdalene, Leonard, and Virgin, with donors and heraldry, south aisle east window; 16th-century panel of Crucifixion, with Virgin and St John, chancel east window.

South Petherwin 15th-century heraldic glass, south aisle window.

CUMBERLAND

Carlisle Cathedral Late-14th-century Doom, east window tracery.

Edenhall Early-14th-century figures of St Cuthbert and King Ceolwyn, east window.

Greystoke 15th-century panels of the life of Saint Andrew, figures of SS Thomas of Canterbury, Oswald, Catherine and the Virgin, with donors, east window; quarries and roundels in chancel south window.

Penrith 15th-century figures of Cicily Neville and Richard, Duke of York, south window.

Wetheral 15th-century figures of saints and donors, west window.

DERBYSHIRE

Ashbourne 13th-century panel of infancy of Christ; 15th-century heraldic glass in north and south transepts.

Caldwell c.1400, two roundels.

Cubley 14th-century figures of St Catherine and another saint, chancel south window.

Dalbury 13th-century figure of St Michael, nave south window.

Dronfield 14th-century musical angels, east window.

Eggington c.1400, Crucifixion, with Virgin and St John, east window; figures of donor and bishop, chancel south.

Haddon Hall chapel 15th-century Crucifixion, with Virgin and St John Baptist, donors and angels, east window; 15th-century figures of St Michael, St Anne and the Virgin and St George, with six figures of apostles and saints in the tracery, north window.

Hault Hucknall 15th-century figures of the Virgin, St John with the Crucifixion, Saint Ursula and donors, with heraldic glass.

Killamarsh 15th-century Pieta, chancel south window.

Morley c.1480, panels of the legend of Robert of Knaresborough, restored; ten panels of the Invention of the True Cross, restored, north aisle windows; 15th-century figures of the Virgin and Child, St Ursula and St Mary Magdalene and the *Te Deum*, north aisle east window; c.1500, figures of SS Peter and Elizabeth with donors, south aisle east window; 15th-century figures of SS William of York, John of Bridlington and Catherine, with Bishop Roger and the four Evangelists, south aisle window.

Norbury 14th-century grisaille, chancel north and south windows; 15th-century figures of SS John Baptist, Barlock Abbas, Anthony and donors, south chapel south window; c.1450, figures of SS Winifrid, Anne and the Virgin and Sitha, with Crucifixion and donors, east window.

Norbury Hall 15th century, six roundels of the Labours of the Months.

Ockbrook c.1500, figures of the four Evangelists, east window.

Sutton in the Dale Armoured donor, north aisle.

West Hallam 15th-century figure of St James the Less, north clerestory window.

DEVONSHIRE

Abbots Bickington 15th-century figures of SS Christopher and Anthony, east window.

Awliscombe c.1500, figures of SS Catherine and Barbara.

Bampton 15th-century figures of the Virgin, St George and the Ascension.

Bere Ferrers c.1338, figures of St James the Great, St Anne and the Virgin, Christ and donors Lord and Lady Ferrers, east window.

Bondleigh 15th-century Annunciation.

Broadwood Kelly c.1523, panels of the Virgin and donors.

Buckland Monachorum 15th-century panels of the life of St Andrew, east window.

Callington 15th-century Virgin and Child, chancel south window tracery.

Calverleigh 14th-century figures of saints, French; 15th-century figures of four Evangelists.

Cockington 15th-century figures of four Apostles.

*Coldridge c.*1480, figure of Prince Edward, east window.

Combe Martin 15th-century figures of seraphim, south window.

Cothele Late-15th-century Crucifixion with St John and the Virgin, chapel east window.

*Doddiscombleigh c.*1450, figures of SS Christopher, Michael, George, Andrew, James the Great and Virgin, with other very restored and modern figures, nave north windows; Seven Sacraments window, with modern figure of Christ, north aisle east window.

Dunsford 15th-century figures of SS Margaret, Barbara, Catherine, Ambrose, with Pope and angels.

*Exeter Cathedral c.*1300, nine saints in main lights; *c.*1392, seven saints in tracery, choir east window; 13th-century grisaille, chapel of St Mary Magdalene; 13th-century grisaille and heraldry, chapel of St Gabriel; *c.*1500, Flemish panels, Lady Chapel.

Hennock 15th-century cherubim, north aisle.

Hempstone Arundel Late-15th-century figure of St Christopher.

Ipplepen Late-15th-century figures of SS Thomas and Brice, east window tracery.

Kelly 15th-century figures of St Edward Confessor, St John Evangelist, the Virgin and Crucifixion, very restored, north chancel aisle.

Kenn 14th-century figures of SS Lucy and John Evangelist, with donor.

Kingskerswell 15th-century figures of SS Apollonia and Peter.

*Littleham c.*1470, figures of SS Michael and Roch, with Christ showing wounds, north aisle window.

Littlehempston SS Stephen and Christopher, with donors, chancel north window.

Lustleigh SS Michael and James. bishop, Virgin and Crucifixion, 15th-century.

Northleigh Late-15th-century figures of SS Peter and James the Great, with bishops, north chapel east window.

Payhembury Late-15th-century figures of SS Blaise, Laurence, Stephen and Vincent.

Sidmouth 15th-century panel of Five Sacred Wounds, in the vestry.

South Sydenham Late-15th-century figures of SS Michael, Mary Magdalene and Sidwell, and the Virgin.

Tor Bryan 15th-century tracery figures.

Yarcombe 15th-century figures of St Paul and a pedlar.

DORSET

Abbotsbury 15th-century part figures of St Catherine and the Virgin.

Athelhampton House 15th-century heraldic glass.

Bradford Abbas 15th-century figures of the Virgin and St John, in vestry.

Bradford Peverell 14th-century panels from New College, Oxford, very restored, east window; 15th-century panels of the Annunciation and Coronation of the Virgin, very restored.

*Cerne Abbas c.*1500, heraldic glass.

Glanvilles Wootton 14th-century figures of saints, south chapel south window.

Loders 15th-century figure of St Leonard of Noblac.

Mapperton 16th-century roundels.

Melbury Bubb 15th-century glass: remains of Seven Sacraments window, Wise and Foolish Virgins, Annunciation, Trinity, Apostles, Evangelist's emblems, heraldry.

Melbury Sampford 15th-century figure of saint.

Melcombe Horsey 15th-century figures of Saints Jerome and Augustine.

Milton Abbey 15th-century figures.

Sherborne Abbey Small 15th-century figures of saints, prophets and heraldry.

Sherborne Hospital Chapel c.1475, restored figures of SS John Evangelist and John Baptist, Virgin and Child, Passion and Evangelist's symbols, Agnus Dei, in south window.

Wimborne Minster Early-16th-century Jesse Tree, damaged, Flemish.

Wimborne St Giles Early-16th-century German glass.

DURHAM

Croft 15th-century glass.

Durham Cathedral Galilee chapel: 14th-century archbishop's head, patterns; 15th-century panels of Crucifixion, Flight into Egypt, Marriage from Seven Sacraments, Apostles, monks; 16th-century death of saint.

Gateshead 13th-century panel of Pilate washing hands, from Tours.

Lanchester Early-14th-century panels of Three Magi, Flight into Egypt and Annunciation.

Raby Castle 15th-century roundels.

ESSEX

Abbess Roding 15th-century figures of SS Margaret and Edmund, chancel south window.

Clavering 15th-century panels of life of St Catherine, Annunciation, seraphim, north aisle east window; SS Apollonia, Sitha, Cecilia, Michael and George, angels and seraphim, north aisle north window; angels and head of Christ, south aisle east window.

Easthorpe c.1530, figure of Christ, Swiss or German, south window.

Great Bardfield Late 14th-century figures of SS Stephen and Laurence. Crucifixion, north aisle windows.

Harlow 14th-century Virgin and Child, north vestry.

Hatfield Peverel 16th-century figures, foreign, south windows.

Heybridge Late-13th-century figure of saint, chancel north window.

Layer Marney Early-16th-century figure of St Peter, heraldry, north chapel east window.

Lindsell 14th-century figures of saints; early-16th-century figures of Virgin and Child, archbishop, donors and heraldry.

Liston 15th-century figures, north window tracery.

Little Baddow c.1400, figure of St Michael, east window.

Margaretting c.1460, Jesse Tree by John Prudde, restored, east window.

Mashbury 14th-century figure of saint, north window.

Netteswell 15th-century figures, north window.

Newport 14th-century figures of SS Michael and Catherine, north transept.

North Ockendon Late-13th-century figure of saint.

Panfield 15th-century figures of saints, nave north window.

Rivenhall 12th-century figures of bishops, French; *c.*1200, panels of Christ, Virgin and Child, Annunciation, Deposition and mounted knight Robert Lemaire; 15th-century figures of bishop, God and three Magi, east window.

Shalford 14th-century heraldic glass, east window.

Sheering Late-14th-century Coronation of the Virgin, with Nine Orders of Angels, east window tracery.

Southend-on-Sea c.1525, many panels of biblical subjects, Flemish or German, south aisle east window.

South Weald Late-15th-century panels, Flemish, west window.

Stambourne c.1530, figures of Henry MacWilliam and wife, with heraldry, east window.

Stapleford Abbots Early-14th-century figure of St Edward the Confessor, north vestry.

Stisted 16th-century fragmentary panels, Flemish, chancel windows.

Thaxted 15th-century figures of SS Laurence and Catherine, bishops, Annunciation and Coronation of the Virgin, nave north aisle tracery; late-14th-century figure of Edmund de Mortimer; 15th-century figure of Abraham, restored, south transept south window; c.1450, panels of Genesis, south aisle windows.

Toppesfield 15th-century panels of Coronation of Virgin, angels, south aisle east window.

White Notley Early-13th-century crowned figure, vestry window.

Woodham Walter 15th-century panels, south aisle window.

GLOUCESTERSHIRE

Abenhall Mid-14th-century figure of St Catherine.

Alstone Small 15th-century figures of Christ, Gabriel and Mass of St Gregory.

Arlingham c.1350, figures of saints, nave north windows; 15th-century figures of saints and apostles, south windows.

Bagenden 15th-century figures of Virgin and SS Catherine and Dorothy, chancel south window; 16th-century figures of SS Margaret and John the Baptist, north aisle windows.

Bledington c.1470, figures of SS Christopher, George, Mary Magdalene, Apostles and donors, Virgin, perhaps by John Prudde.

Bristol Cathedral 14th-century figures.

Bristol, St Mark 15th-century figures.

Bristol, St Mary Redcliffe 15th-century figures.

Buckland c.1475, remains of Seven Sacraments, restored.

Chaceley 14th-century panel.

Chipping Camden 15th-century figures of Apostles and bishops, east window tracery.

Cirencester Late 15th century, many large figures of saints, south aisle south-west window; c.1480, figures of saints and donors, with other 15th-century glass, east window.

Coln Rogers Early-15th-century figure of St Margaret.

Deerhurst c.1450, figures of donors; 15th-century figure of Saint Alphege; c.1320, figure of St Catherine, south aisle west window.

Dymock 15th-century figure. Annunciation.

Dyrrham 15th-century figures, Virgin, SS John Baptist, Evangelist.

Eastington 15th-century figure of St Matthew.

Ebrington 15th-century roundel from Labours of the Months.

Edgeworth c.1360, figure of archbishop.

Fairford c.1500, twenty-eight original windows survive throughout the church.

Frampton-on-Severn Late 15th-century panels, Seven Sacraments, angels.

Gloucester Cathedral c.1350, large east window with many figures of saints, Apostles, angels, kings, bishops and heraldry; c.1480, Jesse Tree remains, saints, kings, Lady Chapel east window; later-15th-century figures of SS John Baptist, Margaret, Oswald, James the Great, Catherine, Dorothy, George, with bishops and angels, nave north windows.

Hailes 15th-century figures of nine Apostles, east window.

Kempsford 15th-century figures of St Anne and Virgin.

Mitcheldean 15th-century musical angels.

Meysey Hampton 14th-century figure of St Michael, south window.

North Cerney Mid-15th-century figures of bishops and Virgin, south transept east window; c.1500, Crucifixion with St John and Virgin, north transept east window; 1470, figures of SS Catherine and Margaret and Virgin and Child.

Northleach 15th-century figures of SS Laurence and Stephen, south aisle.

Notgrove c.1300, Virgin and Child, vestry.

Ozleworth 15th-century figures of four Evangelists, Flemish.

Preston 14th-century Crucifixion in 19th-century window.

Rendcomb c.1520, figures of Christ.

Stanton c.1480, figures from Hailes Abbey.

Sudeley 13th-century panels.

Temple Guiting Late-15th-century figures of Virgin and SS Mary Magdalene and James lesser, nave south window.

Tewkesbury Abbey c.1340, many figures of prophets, kings, knights, choir clerestory windows, north and south; resurrection of the dead, clerestory east windows.

Tortworth 15th-century head of Edward IV, passion shields.

Wick Rissington Early-14th-century Crucifixion.

Winchcombe 15th-century seraphim.

Wormington 15th-century Trinity, musical angel.

HAMPSHIRE

Bentley 15th-century Annunciation.

Bramley Early-16th-century Swiss panels; mid-14th-century figures, north window; 15th-century heraldic glass and musical angels.

Bramshott 15th-century figures.

East Tytherley 13th-century figures.

Froyle 14th-century heraldic glass.

Grateley 13th-century figures of SS Stephen and Gabriel.

Headley 13th-century panel of martyrdom.

Herriard 15th-century figure of St Margaret.

Mottisfont 15th-century Crucifixion, saints (restored), Coronation of Virgin.

Rownhams 16th-century Flemish roundels.

Sherbourne St John Early-16th-century Flemish figures.

Stoke Charity 15th-century figures of St Margaret and the Virgin, very restored.

Winchester Cathedral c.1404, figures of prophets, clerestory; c.1502, figures of saints, Fromond's Chantry; c.1380, very damaged west window.

Winchester, St Cross Late-15th-century figures of SS John, Catherine and Swithin, east window.

Winchester College 15th-century Jesse Tree remains.

HEREFORDSHIRE

Allensmore 14th-century Crucifixion, saint and Angel Gabriel, east window.

Brinsop c.1300, figures of St George and Virgin Mary, with heraldic glass, east window; figure of Christ, north aisle north-west window.

Credenhill c.1310, figures of Archbishop Thomas Cantaur and Bishop Thomas Cantelupe, chancel south window; 14th-century grisaille and heraldic glass, nave north-east window.

Dilwyn 14th-century angels, restored, chancel south window.

Eaton Bishop c.1330, figures of Virgin and Child, Bishop Thomas Cantelupe, SS Michael and Gabriel, Crucifixion and donors, east window; Crucifixion with Virgin and St John, Christ in Majesty and donor figures, chancel south-east window.

Goodrich 15th-century angels, north aisle east window.

Hentland 15th-century figures, east window.

Hereford Cathedral Late-13th-century Christ in Majesty, Crucifixion, bearing of the Cross, Marys at the tomb, grisaille, Evangelist's symbols, Lady Chapel south windows; 14th-century canopies with modern figures, north-east transept; 15th-century figures of SS John Baptist and Elizabeth, bird quarries and St Catherine converting heathen philosophers, north transept west window; early-14th-century figures of SS Mary Magdalene, Ethelbert, Augustine and George, chancel south aisle; 14th-century fragments of story of Joseph, nave south aisle.

Kingsland 14th-century figures of SS Raphael, Michael, Uriel and Gabriel with Virgin, Christ in Majesty, heraldic glass and archbishop, chancel windows.

Ledbury 13th-century medallions, north chapel west window; 15th-century figures in modern east window; c.1500, heraldic glass, north chapel north-east window.

Madley 13th-century medallions of life of Christ, east window; early-14th-century Jesse Tree remains, east window; 14th-century heads and heraldic glass, north-east and south-east windows.

Moccas Early-14th-century canopies, nave north windows; heraldic glass, nave and chancel south windows.

Norton Canon c.1300, grisaille glass, reused in nave south-west and north transept windows.

Pembridge 14th-century figure of St Christopher, restored figures of SS Laurence and Stephen, south aisle west window.

Richards Castle 14th-century Coronation of the Virgin.

Ross on Wye Mid-15th-century figures of SS Edward Confessor, Joachim, Thomas of Hereford and St Anne and the Virgin, east window.

Saint Weonards 15th-century figures of St Catherine and Crucifixion in 19th-century window, north aisle chapel east window; 15th-century figures in tracery, restored; early-16th-century panel, German, nave south window.

Sarnesfield 14th-century, four figures, south transept east window.

Ullingswick 15th-century Virgin and Child, east window.

Weobley 15th-century angels, north window.

Wormbridge Early-15th-century Virgin and Child, massacre of the innocents, chancel windows.

HERTFORDSHIRE

Barkway Late-15th-century remains of Jesse Tree, figures of SS Roch, Sitha and Mary Magdalene and musical angels, south aisle east window.

Barley 14th-century Crucifixion, north aisle east window; 15th-century head of God; 1536, figures, north aisle west window.

Berkhamsted 14th-century heraldic glass, chancel north windows.

Clothall Early-15th-century figures of Christ, Virgin and saints.

Hunsdon c.1445, figures of angels, Resurrection, Ascension, Annunciation, east window; SS John Evangelist, Paul, Peter, Thomas and Andrew, nave north window; fetterlock badges and quarries, chancel south window; bishop and abbot, nave south window.

Much Hadham 15th-century figures of saints, east window.

Royston 15th-century angels, north window.

Saint Pauls Walden Early-14th-century Virgin and Child, tower west window.

Wyddial Mid-16th-century Passion scenes, Flemish, north windows.

HUNTINGDONSHIRE

Diddington 15th-century Pieta.

Kimbolton 15th-century figures.

Tilbrook 16th-century roundels.

Wistow Early-15th-century Resurrection and Annunciation.

Wood Walton Early-15th-century figures.

KENT

Bekesbourne 13th-century grisaille.

Bilsington c.1400, Virgin and Child, Trinity.

Bishopsbourne 14th-century grisaille and angels, chancel north and south windows.

Boughton Aluph Late-14th-century figures of Virgin, Christ, SS Mary Magdalene, Christopher and Margaret, and musical angels, east window tracery; 14th-century heraldic glass, north transept north window.

Brabourne 12th-century grisaille window, chancel north-east window.

Canterbury Cathedral Trinity chapel: nine windows, c.1220, showing the miracles at St Thomas à Becket's tomb and shrine; corona: east window, c.1220, Passion and old Testament scenes, restored; north window, later-12th-century Jesse Tree remains; south window, early-13th-century panel of Christ; north choir aisle: c.1200, two windows of life of Christ and Old Testament scenes; north choir triforium: c.1200, three windows of scenes of lives of Saints Dunstan and Alphege; south choir triforium: early 13th century, three windows of lives of Virgin and Christ; north-east transept north window: c.1178, centre panels of rose window; south choir aisle: 13th century, three windows with French glass; south-west transept south window: c.1178, Old Testament figures; west window: c.1178–90, Old Testament figures; 1396–9, tracery figures of Apostles and angels; mid-15th-century figures of kings and Apostles with heraldic glass; nave north-west window: 15th-century figure of St Edward the Confessor; north-west transept north window: 1476–80, figures of Royal family; Apostles and saints in tracery; north-east transept east window: 1220, figure of Saint Martin; clerestory, c.1178, Old Testament figures; Water Tower windows: 13th-century figures of Apostles; 15th-century figures of archbishops; crypt: chapel of Saint Mary Magdalene, 13th-century panel of Anointing of Christ's feet; Chapel of St Nicholas, 13th-century panels of life of St Nicholas; east window, 13th-century panels; chapel of St Gabriel, 13th-, 14th- and 15th-century panels; south aisle, 14th-century figures of SS Christopher and John Baptist.

Canterbury, St Mildred 15th-century figures.

Canterbury, St Peter 14th-century heraldic glass, north aisle window.

*Chartham c.*1294, panels of Christ in Majesty, Coronation of the Virgin and grisaille, chancel windows.

Chilham Mid-15th-century figures of saints and angels, nave windows.

*Cranbrooke c.*1520, figures of St George, etc., north aisle windows.

*Crundale c.*1300, Coronation of the Virgin, restored.

Ditton 14th-century angels.

Doddington 13th-century medallion of Flight into Egypt, south chapel.

East Malling Late-15th-century Coronation of the Virgin.

East Sutton 15th-century figures of SS Peter and Paul, west window.

Elham 15th-century figure of St Thomas à Becket and heraldic glass; 16th-century Netherland roundels.

Eynesford 15th-century Crucifixion.

Faversham Saint Catherine 13th-century grisaille glass.

Fawkham 13th-century grisaille; 14th-century figure of Virgin, west window.

Fordwich 14th-century panels.

Goodnestone 14th-century figures of St Michael and archbishops.

Great Chart Late-15th-century figures of SS Michael and George, musical angels and donors, east window, south chapel.

Harbledown 15th-century angels, east window; 14th-century grisaille, 15th-century figures, chancel north window; 14th-century Ascension panel, chancel south window.

Hastingleigh 13th-century grisaille glass.

Headcorn 15th-century figures of saints.

High Halden 15th-century angels.

Hoo, St Werburgh 15th-century angels, east window, north aisle.

*Iwade c.*1540, Crucifixion, restored.

Kemsing 13th-century Virgin and Child, nave south window: 15th-century figures of St Anne and St John Baptist, east window.

Kennington 13th-century grisaille glass, chancel windows.

Kingsdown 14th-century Virgin and Child, nave north window; 14th-century figure of Christ, nave window.

*Kingsnorth c.*1400, figure of St Michael.

Leeds 15th-century figure of St Nicholas.

Leigh 14th-century Virgin.

Lullingstone 14th-century figures of bishops, north chapel window; 15th-century figures of SS Erasmus and George, nave north-west window; early-16th-century figures of SS Agnes, Elizabeth and Anne with Virgin Mary, with heraldic glass, east window.

Meopham 15th-century figures of St Catherine and bishop.

Mersham 15th-century figures of SS Christopher and George, and archbishop, chancel south window.

Nackington Early-13th-century Jesse Tree, Marriage at Cana and St Thomas à Becket, chancel north window.

*Nettlestead c.*1438, figures of SS Stephen and Laurence, chancel north window; 15th-century figures of Apostles and heraldic glass, nave north window; 15th-century scenes of St Thomas à Becket, east window.

Offham 15th-century angels and heraldic glass, chancel windows.

Sandhurst 15th-century figures of St Michael, priest and abbess, south window.

Selling 1299–1307, figures of SS John, Mary Magdalene, Virgin and Child, Margaret, with heraldic glass and grisaille, east window.

Sevington 14th-century figure of Virgin.

Snodland 15th-century figure of St James, west window.

Stodmarsh 13th-century grisaille glass, chancel north window.

Stowting Early 14th-century Virgin and Child; *c.*1460, figures of SS James Great, John the Baptist and Augustine, with donors, nave south window.

*Upchurch c.*1300, figure of angel, east window.

*Upper Hardres c.*1200, figures of Virgin and Child, St Nicholas and donors; early-14th-century figures of St Anne and Virgin, Saint Elizabeth and Virgin, St Edmund and other saints, with heraldic glass, east window.

*Warehorne c.*1300, grisaille glass with figures, north aisle window.

*Westwell c.*1245, Jesse Tree remains, Virgin and Christ only original, the remainder modern restoration, east window.

*West Wickham c.*1500, Virgin and Child, St Anne and Virgin, St Christopher and donor, Lady Chapel east window; SS Dorothy, Catherine and Christopher, with Virgin, north windows.

Willesborough Early-14th-century figures of SS Margaret and John Baptist, chancel north window; 15th-century figures of Virgin and Child, John the Baptist, Holy Spirit and seraphim, south aisle east window.

Wingham Early-14th-century grisaille glass.

Woodchurch 13th-century medallion of Dormition of Virgin, nave south window.

Wormshill Late-14th-century Coronation of Virgin.

Wye 15th-century heraldic glass.

LANCASHIRE

*Ashton-under-Lyne c.*1480, four windows depicting the life of St Helena, nave south windows.

Beckside 14th-century figure of Christ, chancel window.

Cartmel Fell 15th-century Seven Sacraments window; late-14th-century St Anthony, etc., St Anthony's Chapel east window.

Cartmel Priory Mid-15th-century figures of Virgin and Child, SS John the Baptist, Peter, Andrew, Bartholomew and Matthias, east window.

*Denton c.*1500, figures, chancel north and south.

Eccles Early-16th-century panel of Entry to Jerusalem, Flemish, south aisle west window.

Halsall 14th-century grisaille panels, north aisle west window; angels, south aisle east window.

Middleton 1524, figures of seventeen archers, chancel south.

St Michael on Wyre Early-14th-century heraldic glass.

Sefton Late-15th-century Passion symbols, south aisle east window.

Tunstall Late-15th-century Flemish figure of Virgin; 16th-century figures of Christ and St Peter, east window.

LEICESTERSHIRE

Appleby Magna Late-14th-century angels and figures.

*Ayston c.*1480, Crucifixion, Adoration of Magi, Presentation at the Temple, south aisle windows.

*Coleorton c.*1500, figures of saints and priests, French, tower window.

Coston 14th-century Crucifixion.

Garthorpe 14th-century figures of saints.

Launde Abbey c.1450, many figures of saints.

Leicester: Newark House c.1500–1520, figures of SS Margaret, Christopher, Catherine and George, and Nativity.

Leicester: Old Jewry Museum c.1500–1520, Seven Sacraments panels, Acts of Mercy panels, Life of Virgin and Passion scenes.

North Luffenham 14th-century figures of SS Mary Magdalene, Barbara and Edward the Confessor, and heraldic glass, chancel windows.

Peckleton 14th-century figures of St Michael and a nun, chancel.

Ratby 15th-century angels.

Rothley 15th-century figure of donor, south aisle window.

Skeffington Late-15th-century figures of Virgin and donors, east window.

Stockerston 15th-century figures of SS Clement and Christopher, donors, Crucifixion, north windows.

Thornton 14th-century panels of life of Christ, south aisle window.

Thurcaston 14th- and 15th-century figures including donor, east window.

Twycross Mid-12th-century Presentation at Temple; c.1245, Moses, Solomon and other panels, French glass, east window.

Withcote Hall chapel 1530–40, figures of SS Bartholomew, Simon, Thomas, James, Andrew, Christopher and Peter, with Christ, David, Joel and Daniel.

Whitwell 14th-century Crucifixion, chancel window.

Witherley 15th-century Virgin.

LINCOLNSHIRE

Addlethorpe 15th-century angels, priests, south windows.

Barnoldby le Beck 14th-century Virgin, St John and Crucifixion, south aisle east window.

Boston Guildhall 15th-century figures of Apostles.

Carlton Scroop c.1370, heraldic donors, east window.

Corby 15th-century figures of Virgin and St John, north aisle window.

Croxton Early-14th-century Crucifixion, south window.

Edenhall 15th-century figure of St Catherine.

Edenham 15th-century angels and saints, south aisle windows; St Catherine, north aisle west window.

Gedney Early-14th-century Jesse Tree remains.

Heydour c.1380, figures of SS Edward the Confessor, George and Edmund; 14th-century figure of St Laurence; 15th-century figures of SS Stephen and Vincent, north aisle windows.

Kelby 14th-century figures, south aisle east window.

Kingerby 15th-century figures of St Catherine, etc., south aisle east window.

Lea c.1330, Crucifixion and figure of Bishop Grosseteste, chantry east window.

Lincoln Cathedral South transept windows: 12th- and 13th-century panels; south transept rose window: 13th-century glass; south aisle east window: 13th-century panels; north aisle east window: 13th-century panels; north transept windows: 13th-century grisaille glass; north transept rose window: early-13th-century glass.

Long Sutton c.1370, figure, south chancel aisle.

Lynwood 15th-century figure of bishop, chancel south window.

Messingham 14th-and 15th-century figures in south aisle east window and elsewhere.

Metheringham 15th-century figures of Apostles in clerestory.

North Thoresby 15th-century figures.

Pinchbeck 15th-century figures in north aisle tracery.

Stamford, St George 15th-century figures of SS Anne and Catherine, chancel south; 1450, 'Garter' window, chancel.

Stamford, St John 15th-century figures of SS Edmund, Blaise, Peter, Leonard, etc.

Stamford, St Martin 15th-century figures and biblical scenes, chancel and nave windows.

Stragglethorpe 13th-century medallion.

Tattershall c.1481, Acts of Mercy, Seven Sacraments, Virtues, SS James, Peter and John, musical angels, east window.

Wrangle 1345–71, Jesse Tree figures, SS George, Cecilia, Laurence, Edmund, John, Peter, Lucy, Barbara, Stephen, Edward the Confessor and Virgin, north aisle windows.

LONDON

Victoria and Albert Museum 13th- to 16th-century glass from England and the Continent.

Westminster Abbey 13th-century panels of martyrdoms of SS John the Baptist, Stephen and Nicholas and life of Christ, Jerusalem Chamber.

MIDDLESEX

Greenford c.1500, heraldic glass, chancel windows.

Harefield 16th-century figures of Christ, Apostles and saints, north chapel east window.

Perivale 15th-century figures of SS Matthew and John the Baptist, east window.

South Mimms 1526, figures of donors.

Tottenham, All Hallows Late-16th-century French figures of Evangelists and Prophets, north aisle window.

NORFOLK

Ashill 15th-century figures of SS Gregory, John, Matthew, Jerome and Augustine, north windows.

Attleborough 14th-century angels and heraldic glass, west window.

Bale 15th-century Annunciation panels, angels; 14th-century figures of prophets, nave south window.

Banningham 15th-century Annunciation, north aisle window.

Bawburgh 15th-century figures of angels, St Barbara, south window.

Bedingham 15th-century figures of SS Philip and Paul, north aisle windows.

Brundall 16th-century Flemish roundel of St Laurence.

Burnham Deepdale 15th-century figure of St Mary Magdalene.

Carlton Rode 13th-century figure in trefoil, chancel south window.

Castle Acre 15th-century figure of St George, south aisle east window.

Cawston 15th-century musical angels, south aisle window.

Chedgrave 16th-century figures of angels and saints, foreign, east window.

Cley 15th-century figures of SS Agatha, Sitha, Petronilla, Faith, Apollonia, Cecilia and Christ, south aisle windows.

Denton 15th-century roundels; 16th-century foreign heraldic glass.

Diss 15th-century Virgin and Child, St Mary Magdalene and heads of saints, north aisle west window.

Dunston 14th-century figures of SS Christopher and Remigius, with donor; early-16th-century saint, chancel window.

Earsham Early-16th-century foreign panels, east and south windows.

East Harling c.1480, fifteen panels of life and Passion of Christ, with donors, east window; 15th-century angels and heraldic glass, south aisle east window; 15th-century angels, clerestory north windows.

Elsing c.1330, Virgin and heraldic glass; c.1375, figures of Apostles, chancel south windows.

Emneth 15th-century figures of angels, Virgin and Saints Cuthbert and Scytha, north aisle windows.

Erpingham 15th- and 16th-century Flemish panels, east window.

Field Dalling 15th-century figures in north and south windows.

Framingham Earl 15th-century figures of SS Margaret and Catherine.

Great Cressingham 15th-century figures of angels, saints and bishops, north aisle windows.

Great Snoring 15th-century angels in chancel windows.

Griston 15th-century figures of St Catherine, Prophets and angels, south windows.

Guestwick 15th-century figures, south aisle.

Halvergate Early-14th-century figure of St Christopher, north window.

Harpley 15th-century figures of saints and angels, west window.

Hingham c.1500, figures of St Andrew, St Anne and the Virgin and donors, Crucifixion, Deposition, Ascension and Resurrection, German, east window.

Kelling 14th-century figures, chancel window.

Ketteringham 15th-century figures, east window.

Kimberley 15th-century figures of SS Catherine, Margaret and John; 14th-century figures of John the Baptist, angels, archbishop and Crucifixion, east and south-east windows.

Langley 16th century, four panels of French glass, east window.

Letheringsett 15th-century panels, chancel south-west window.

Long Stratton Late-15th-century panel of Baptism of Christ, French, east window.

Martham 15th-century figures of SS Edmund, Margaret, Juliana, Agnes and Virgin and Child, with Annunciation, Ascension, Resurrection, Crucifixion, Mocking of Christ (Flemish), Edward III and Queen Philippa and angels, north aisle east window; 15th-century figures of SS John, James the Great, Margaret and Michael, with angels, Eve spinning, south aisle east window.

Mileham c.1350, figures of SS Margaret, Catherine, John the Baptist, etc., west window; 15th-century figures of SS Margaret and John, with bishop, east window; 15th-century figures of donors, chancel south window.

Mulbarton 15th-century figures of Adam, king, bishop, angels, Expulsion from Eden, east window; 15th-century musical angels, king; 16th-century nun and monk, Flemish, chancel south window.

Narborough 15th-century angels, chancel north window.

North Elmham 14th-century figures of Virgin and Child and musical angels, south aisle window.

North Tuddenham 15th-century panels of lives of SS Margaret and George, and figures of saints, west tower window.

Norwich : Cathedral 15th-century pieces including figures of king, angels, heraldic glass, Baptism of Christ, north choir ambulatory; 15th-century Virgin and Child, south choir chapel; 16th-century figure of St Brice, French, south choir ambulatory.

Norwich: St James 16th-century Flemish panels.

Norwich: St Peter Hungate 15th-century figures, including SS John, Agatha, James Great, Andrew and Apostles, with angels, east window; 15th-century angels, chancel north window; 15th-century angels, St Peter and Christ, chancel north windows; 15th-century angels, Virgin and Christ, west window.

Norwich: St Peter Mancroft Later-15th-century, forty-two panels of life of Christ; death of the Virgin, story of St Peter; figures of SS John, Francis, Margaret, and Cecilia, donors, and many saints in the tracery, east window.

Norwich: St Stephen 1511, panels from Germany, east window.

Outwell Early-16th-century figures, south chapel east window; figure, north chapel north window.

Plumstead 15th-century figures, east window; 16th-century angel, south window.

Poringland 14th-century Passion symbols, Gabriel, Risen Christ, chancel east window.

Pulham St Mary 14th-century Christ and angels, nave north-east window; 15th-century, twelve figures including SS Cecilia, Catherine, Mary Magdalene, Barbara, Peter and Andrew, chancel window.

Ringland 15th-century figures of Virgin and Child, Trinity, Annunciation, John the Baptist and donors, clerestory windows.

Salle 15th-century figures of Orders or Angels, prophets and patriarchs, SS Jerome, Margaret, Catherine, Etheldreda, Helen, Virgin Mary, Christ, musical angels and donors, east window and south transept south window.

Saxlingham Nethergate 13th-century medallions of martyrdoms, St Edmund and Apostles James and John; 13th-century grisaille panel; 14th-century figures of Apostles Philip and James; 15th-century pieces including Resurrection, chancel south window; 15th-century Pentecost, Ascension, Coronation of Virgin, heraldic glass, east window; 15th-century figures of SS Jerome and Ambrose, angels, chancel north window; 15th-century figures of Edward the Confessor, archbishop, bishop and musical angels, north chapel east window.

Seething 15th-century heraldic angel, chancel north window.

Shelton Early-16th-century figures of Virgin, angels and heraldic donors, east window; early-16th-century Annunciation, Resurrection and angel, north aisle east window; early-16th-century donors of Shelton family, south aisle east window.

Shimpling 15th-century musical angels, north and south windows.

South Acre Late-13th-century grisaille glass, north chapel east window.

South Creake 15th-century figures of SS Agatha, Helena, and James Great, Trinity, donors and angels, north and south windows.

Stody 15th-century Jesse Tree figures of kings, and SS Matthias, Philip, Bartholomew and Virgin, nave north and south transept east windows.

Stradsett 1540, Adoration of the Magi, South German, and Crucifixion, west window.

Stratton Strawless 15th-century figures of SS Catherine, Helena, Matthew, Mark, Luke and John, musical angel, Coronation of Virgin and Annunciation, north windows.

*Taverham c.*1450, Crucifixion with Virgin and St John, donors and angels, north aisle window.

Thurton 15th-century Trinity.

Warham St Mary 1450–75, musical angels and heads; early-14th-century Adam and Eve, nave north window; 16th-century Lower Rhenish glass of Passion scenes, monks, David, Christ, etc.

Weston Longueville 15th-century figures of St Philip and musical angels, restored, south aisle windows.

Wiggenhall St Mary Late-15th-century figures of over forty saints, with angels, tracery of nave north windows.

Woodton 14th-century figures of SS Margaret and Catherine, with Passion symbols, south aisle east window.

NORTHAMPTONSHIRE

Aldwinkle c.1290, figures of SS George and Christopher, south window; 15th-century figures of priests, east window.

Cranford Saint Andrew 15th-century figure, east window.

Great Brington 1532, figures including St John the Baptist, chancel south window.

Holdenby 13th-century Coronation of the Virgin, chancel south window.

Lowick c.1330–40, Jesse Tree, sixteen figures of kings and prophets, and saints including SS John the Baptist, Andrew and Michael, north aisle windows; c.1380, figure of knight, north aisle window; heraldic glass in south chancel and north chantry windows.

Newton Bromhold 15th-century figure of archbishop, north aisle window.

Rushden Late-15th-century remains of Jesse Tree, east window.

Stanford on Avon Early-14th-century figures of Virgin, saints, donors, crucifixion, east window; 14th-century figures of Apostles, saints, Virgin and Christ, chancel side windows; 1330–40, Resurrection, Crucifixion, St Anne, bishop, angels, north aisle east window; 1330–40, figures of saints, south aisle east window; c.1500, figure of Virgin, Visitation, SS John, Margaret, George, donors in south-east and west windows; c.1558, figures of Cave family, east window.

Thenford Early-15th-century figure of St Peter.

NORTHUMBERLAND

Blanchland Abbey 15th-century figures of canons, east windows.

Bothal 14th-century Annunciation.

Morpeth 14th-century Jesse Tree, heavily restored, east window; 14th-century figures of Christ, SS Blaise and Denys, angels and grotesques, south aisle east window.

Newcastle Cathedral 15th-century Virgin and Child, north transept east aisle window.

Ponteland 14th-century figure of priest.

Stannington Early-14th-century figure and heraldic glass, vestry.

NOTTINGHAMSHIRE

Annesley 15th-century heraldic glass.

Averham 15th-centure figures, chancel north window.

Cossall Early-15th-century St Catherine.

Cropwell Bishop Late-14th-century figure, north aisle east window.

East Markham 15th-century figures including Saint Scytha and heraldic glass, south aisle windows.

Egmanton c.1360, figures of SS George and Michael, south transept window.

Fledborough 14th-century figures of Virgin and Child, SS John the Baptist and Andrew, knight and grisaille.

Halam Late-14th-century figures of SS Anthony and Christopher, and Adam and Eve, south-west window.

Lambley Late-14th-century Virgin, and Virgin and Child; 15th-century Crucifixion, east window.

Low Marnham 15th-century figure of St James, north window.

Newark 15th-century remains of Seven Deadly Sins, Passion symbols, saints, panels from life and Passion of Christ, musical angels, donors, heraldic glass; c.1310, panels of Creation, Expulsion from Eden, Agony in Garden, Adoration of Magi, Scourging of Christ, Marys at the Tomb, heraldic glass, south aisle east window.

Nuthall 15th-century Crucifixion with Virgin and St John, and heraldic glass, east window.

Papplewick 15th-century figures of SS Stephen and Peter, with donor and priests, south window.

Southwell Minster c.1300, knight, Adoration of Magi, chapter house windows.

Strelley 14th-century figure, 16th-century figures, north windows.

Tuxford c.1500, figure of St Laurence.

Woodborough 15th-century figures of SS Margaret, Catherine, etc.

OXFORDSHIRE

Aston Rowant Mid-14th-century figure of Christ, north aisle east window; 15th-century figure of Christ and musical angel, north aisle window.

Beckley Early-14th-century Assumption of Virgin, chancel east window; mid-14th-century Coronation and Assumption of Virgin, chancel north window; mid-14th-century figure of St Edmund, nave north window; later-14th-century figures of SS James Great and Christopher, mid-15th-century figure of St Anne and Virgin, west window.

Begbroke Mid-15th-century half-figure of God, chancel south window, 16th-century and later roundels, Flemish, chancel south window; 16th-century Flemish panels of bishop and Tobit and the Fish, nave north window.

Brightwell Baldwin 14th-century restored figures of SS Peter and Paul; early-15th-century figures of Saint Paul and the Virgin and heraldic glass; chancel north windows; early-15th- century Crucifixion, vestry east window; mid-14th-century saint and Annunciation; 15th-century Annunciation and heraldic glass, chancel south windows.

Burford 15th-century figures of SS George, Margaret, Barbara, Mary Magdalene and seraphim, nave west window; 15th-century figures of SS John the Baptist, Christopher, Gabriel and Apostle, chancel east window.

Cassinton 14th-century roundels of deacons; 16th-century roundel of life of Joseph, Flemish, north window.

Charlton-on-Otmoor 13th-century Virgin and Child, chancel east window.

Chinnor Mid-14th-century remains of Acts of Mercy series, and figures of SS Laurence and Alban, bishop and archbishop, chancel north and south windows; 14th-century Christ in Majesty with angels, and heraldic glass, north aisle windows.

Combe 15th-century Coronation of Virgin, with angels, east window; 15th-century figure of St James the Great and cherubim, restored, nave south and north windows.

Dorchester Abbey Mid-13th-century panel of St Birinus, chancel chapel east window; c.1300–1320, heraldic glass, south-east chancel window; c.1320, figures of SS Birinus, Laurence, Michael, Virgin and Child, Annunciation, Christ in

Above: 'St Michael', detail,
Norwich school, mid-
fifteenth century – Martham,
Norfolk; *below:* 'Virgin and
Child', detail, later-fifteenth
century – Woolley,
Yorkshire

Left : St Thomas à Becket',
by John Prudde, *c.* 1447 –
Warwick St Mary,
Warwickshire; *right :* 'Sir
Robert Clifford', Norwich
school, *c.* 1480 – Long
Melford, Suffolk

Majesty, remains of Doom and donors, east window; c.1320, Jesse Tree remains, north-east chancel window; early-14th-century heraldic glass, nave north windows; mid-14th-century Mass, c.1300, roundels, sedilia head window.

Drayton Saint Leonard Mid-14th-century figure of St Leonard, restored, chancel north window.

Ewelme 14th-century censing angel, 15th-century figures of SS Mark and Andrew, heraldic glass, chancel chapel east window.

Eynsham Early-15th-century figure of St Thomas, south aisle window.

Great Milton Early-14th-century scenes of life of Lazarus, north aisle east window.

Hampton Poyle c.1400–1430, Evangelist's symbols, chancel north window.

Hardwick (near Bicester) Mid-14th-century figures of St John the Baptist and Christ, restored, east window.

Heythrop Early-16th-century figures of SS Matthew, Mark, Luke, John, Virgin and Christopher, east window; 1522, Ashefield donor and wife, south window.

Horley c.1420, donor figures of two rectors, north aisle windows.

Horspath c.1300, figures of Virgin and St John Evangelist; 15th-century figure of archbishop, chancel south window; late-15th-century Crucifixion, chancel north window.

Iffley Late-15th-century angels and heraldic glass, nave north windows.

Kelmscott c.1450–80, figure of St George, east window.

Kidlington 13th-century remains of Jesse Tree; 1300, Crucifixion; 15th-century figures including Saint Frideswide, Virgin and Child, St Anne and Virgin, and heraldic glass, east window; 14th- and 15th-century heraldic glass, chancel south window.

Lower Heyford 14th-century figure of Christ; c.1471–90, heraldic glass, south aisle west window.

Mapledurham Late-15th-century figures of SS Stephen, Zita and Mary Magdalene and heraldic glass, east window.

Marsh Baldon c.1365, figures of Virgin and St John, St Anne and Virgin, angels and heraldic glass.

Minster Lovell c.1455–85, figures of Isaac and Daniel, St Agnes, etc., chancel north and south windows; figure of Saint Lucy, north transept north window; figures of St Peter Martyr and friar, nave north window; figure of doctor saint, nave south window.

Newington c.1482–1511, Assumption of Virgin and Trinity, with donor priests, chancel north window.

North Leigh c.1440, remains of alphabet design, Wilcote chantry windows.

Oxford

    All Souls College: 1441–47, much glass in the windows of the antechapel; east window: figures of Apostles and saints; south-west window: figures of kings of England and saints; north-west window: figures of bishops and doctors; north door window: kings and saints.

    Balliol College: East window, 1529, Passion scenes; south side east window, 1529, Legend of Saint Catherine; south side, second from east, 16th-century figures; north side, third from east, 16th-century figures; north side, fourth from east, c.1529–30, figures; upper library windows, late-15th-century heraldic glass.

    Christ Church Cathedral: Chapel of St Lucy: east window, 14th-century figures and grotesques; Latin Chapel: mid-14th-century figures in three north windows; Chapter House: late-15th- and early-16th-century panels in north and south windows.

Merton College: East window: 14th-century figures, 15th-century heraldic glass and *c.*1290, figures in tracery; choir north and south windows: *c.*1290, grisaille glass with figures of saints and donor Henry Mamesfield; crossing west window: 15th-century figures of saints.

New College: Antechapel north and south windows: late-14th-century figures of saints, angels, prophets and ecclesiatics; hall staircase: 14th-century heraldic glass.

Oriel College: Antechapel north-west window: early-16th-century figure of St Margaret.

The Queen's College: Chapel windows: 1518, figures and heraldic glass.

Trinity College: Old Library east windows: mid-15th-century figures of saints and Evangelists; Old Library south window; 15th-century heraldic glass and 16th-century Flemish roundels; Durham Quad side room, first floor, east window: 14th-century grotesques and 15th-century figures.

Saint Ebbe: South aisle window: 15th-century heraldic glass.

Saint Michael: Chancel east window: late-13th-century figures of Virgin and Child and SS Nicholas, Michael and Edmund of Abingdon; north aisle north-east window: early-15th-century seraphim and Annunciation with Lily Crucifix.

Saint Peter-in-the-East: Chancel east window: *c.*1500, Crucifixion, SS Christopher, Dorothy, Elizabeth and Virgin and Child; north chapel north window: mid-15th-century figures of SS Vincent, Paul and Peter, Virgin and Christ in Majesty.

Shiplake 15th-century French glass figures including SS Anthony Abbot, John Evangelist, Barbara, Peter, Catherine, Omer, John the Baptist, Vision of Peter of Luxembourg, Christ and seraphim, east window; figures and fragments, south aisle windows; Evangelist's symbols and figures, west window.

South Leigh 15th-century remains including Adam and heads, chancel north chapel east window.

South Newington Late-13th-century heraldic glass, south aisle windows; early-14th-century Evangelist's symbols, chancel windows; early-14th-century grotesques, north aisle windows.

South Stoke Late-13th-century Virgin and Child, south aisle east window.

*Stanton Harcourt c.*1250–80, grisaille glass with figure of St James the Great, chancel south windows; mid-13th-century panels of a bishop and king; *c.*1475, heraldic glass, Harcourt Chapel south window.

Stanton Saint John Late-13th-century panel of Funeral of the Virgin, with angels and heraldic glass, chancel south window; late-13th-century grisaille glass, restored, chancel north windows; mid-14th-century grotesque, tower west window.

Stonesfield 15th-century Evangelist's symbols and other remains, chancel east window; late-15th-century heraldic glass, tower west window; mid-16th-century heraldic glass, chancel south window; mid-16th-century heraldic glass, nave south clerestory.

Tadmarton Late-13th-century head of Christ, north aisle east window.

*Waterperry c.*1260, grisaille glass, chancel north windows; early-14th-century Christ in Majesty and donor figures, nave north window; 1461–9 donor figures, restored, nave north window; *c.*1530, donor figures and heraldic glass, south window.

*Waterstock c.*1500, donor figures, north aisle window.

*Westwell c.*1522, remains of Crucifixion, and donors, nave south window.

Wolvercote Early-14th-century grisaille glass, chancel south window.

Yarnton Late-15th-century figures of Virgin, Apostle and angels, east window; *c.*1500, bird quarries, chancel north window; late-15th- and early-16th-century Flemish roundels and *c.*1400–1430, figures of SS Thomas à Becket and Nicholas, with donor monks, nave north window; *c.*1400–1430, panels of St Christopher and Virgin and Child, nave north window; *c.*1300, donor figure; 15th-century figure of Saint John Baptist; *c.*1530, figure of St Thomas, nave north window.

SHROPSHIRE

Alderbury 14th-century Virgin and angels, south aisle window.

Alveley 15th-century figures including a bishop, south clerestory windows.

*Atcham c.*1488, Virgin and Child, St John, God the Father, angels and donors, east window.

Badger 16th-century Flemish figures of Christ and saints.

Battlefield 16th-century French figures, vestry window; mid-15th-century figure of saint.

Bromfield 16th-century Flemish roundels, vestry window.

Church Stretton 16th-century Flemish roundels, chancel north and south windows.

Coalbrookdale 16th-century Flemish panels including the Last Supper.

Diddlebury 14th-century Crucifixion.

Donington 15th-century figures of Virgin and Christ, east window.

Eyton 15th-century figure of St Catherine.

Hughley 14th-century figure of Virgin, chancel north window; early-15th-century figures, east window.

Kinlet 14th-century figures including knights and saints, east window.

Ludlow 14th-century Jesse Tree, Lady Chapel east window; *c.*1445, panels of six Commandments, chancel south window; later-15th-century figures of SS Paul, Luke, Helena, Elizabeth, James the Great, Joseph of Glastonbury, James lesser, Catherine, Etheldreda and Margaret, with smaller figures in tracery, chancel south window; *c.*1445, twenty-seven panels of life of St Laurence, with many figures of saints in the tracery, east window; later-15th-century figures of SS George, Mary Magdalene, Leonard, Dunstan, John of Bridlington, Apollonia, Stephen, Thomas Becket, Laurence, Catherine, Edward Confessor, Vincent, Helena and Augustine, with musical angels and figures in tracery, chancel north windows; *c.*1470, Legend of Saint Edward Confessor and Saint John, eight panels, St John's Chapel east window; later-15th-century figures of Twelve Apostles with Creed, Saint John's Chapel north windows; later-15th-century figures of Christ, Annunciation, and SS Catherine, Christopher and John the Baptist, St John's Chapel north window.

Morville Early-14th-century Crucifixion, north aisle east window.

Munslow 14th-century Virgin and Child, St John and priest donor, nave south window; 16th-century Crucifixion.

*Prees c.*1440, fragments including many heads; *c.*1500, figure of knight, restored.

Shawbury 15th-century figure of priest and head of Virgin, chancel south window.

*Shrewsbury, Saint Mary c.*1340, Jesse Tree, very restored, with figures of donors, and saints in tracery, east window; *c.*1500, many panels of life of St Bernard, Flemish, chancel north windows; *c.*1500, Flemish panels of Presentation, St Peter with donors and Crucifixion, nave south window; *c.*1475, figures of SS Agatha, Bartholomew, Peter, James the Great, and Lambert with donors, German, from Trèves, nave north window; *c.*1475, figures of SS Sebastian and Jerome, with donors, German, nave north window; 16th-century figures of SS Catherine and

Barbara, St Anne and the Virgin with donors, Flemish, Trinity chapel south window.

Stottesdon 14th-century heraldic glass, and head of knight.

Tong 15th-century figures including SS James, John with Salome, St Mary Magdalene, Annunciation, SS Edmund and Peter, Virgin and Child, Evangelist's symbols and angels, east window.

Upton Cresset 16th-century Flemish panel.

Worfield 14th-century Crucifixion, very restored, south aisle east window.

SOMERSET

Alford Early-16th-century figure of St Mary Magdalene.

Banwell 15th-century scene from life of St Nicholas, with figures of priests and bishops, south aisle east window; 15th-century figure of bishop, north aisle east window.

Bishops Lydeard 15th-century remains including part of Baptism from Seven Sacraments, heads, etc., vestry window.

Broomfield 15th-century figures including angels and donor, Passion symbols and heraldic glass, chancel south-west window.

Brushford Early-16th-century Virgin, French, chancel south window.

Brympton D'Evercy c.1340, Virgin; 15th-century remains of four saints, west window and north chapel.

Buckland Denham 15th-century Evangelist's symbols, chapel window.

Burnham-on-Sea 15th-century heraldic glass.

Burrington 15th-century remains of Seven Sacraments and figures, north window.

Butcombe 15th-century figure and Passion symbols, south chancel chapel east window.

Butleigh 15th-century heraldic glass and remains of figures.

Charlinch 15th-century figures of SS Sitha, Catherine, Apollinia and Cecilia, south transept east window.

Cheddar 15th-century figures of SS Barbara and John, Annunciation, Evangelist's symbols, much heraldic glass, St Nectan's Chapel, east and south windows.

Chelwood 16th-century Flemish glass including St Agatha, south aisle windows.

Chewton Mendip 15th-century figures of Virgin, SS Sidwell and Margaret and heraldic glass, vestry window.

Churchill 15th-century glass from Wakefield Cathedral, including figures of St Catherine, musical angels and Risen Christ, north windows.

Claverton Early-14th-century panel of Betrayal, German (it may be a careful 19th-century copy), north transept window.

Clevedon, Christ Church 13th-century figure of king from Jesse Tree, French; 16th-century Coronation of Virgin, Risen Christ, carpenter, Flemish; 14th-century Virgin, prophets and angels, French, east window.

Compton Bishop c. 1375, figures of Trinity, God, SS Peter, Catherine, Gabriel and Paul, east window tracery.

Cothelstone 15th-century figures of SS Thomas of Hereford and Thomas à Becket, restored, north chapel windows.

Croscombe 15th-century remains of saints, south aisle east window.

Curry Mallet 15th-century figure of saintly doctor, north aisle east window.

Curry Rivel 13th-century panel from Canterbury; 15th-century figure of saint, south aisle window, behind organ; 15th-century figures of saints and angels, north aisle window.

Dinder 15th-century panels of St Michael, Trinity and remains of Crucifixion, pulpit window, south side.

Ditcheat 15th-century angels with Passion symbols, south transept east window.

East Brent Late-15th-century glass, considerably restored: Passion scenes, east window north aisle; SS James the Great, John the Evangelist and John the Baptist, and seraphim, north aisle window.

East Coker 15th-century heraldic glass, south transept window.

Farleigh Hungerford, St Leonard 15th-century figures of SS Leonard, Christopher, Elizabeth with John the Baptist, Anthony and Cecilia, and angels, east window; angels, chancel north and south windows; head of Sir Thomas Hungerford, north window.

Farleigh Hungerford Castle, St Leonard's Chapel 16th-century and later panels from Netherlands and Germany.

Glastonbury, St John's 15th-century figures of SS Catherine and John Evangelist, Annunciation, Virgin, angels and donors, chancel north window; 15th-century figures of St Dunstan, angels, donors, heraldic glass, chancel south window.

Glastonbury, St Patrick's Chapel 15th-century remains of Visiting the Prisoners, from Seven Sacraments.

Halse 16th-century Flemish enamelled glass, east window.

Hatch Beauchamp 15th-century figures of Virgin, St Paul and angel, north windows.

High Ham 15th-century figures of St Luke and bishop, east window; 15th-century figure of Abraham, chancel south window; 15th-century Trinity symbol, nave south aisle window.

Huish Champflower 15th-century Jesse Tree remains, north chapel east window.

Hutton c.1500 heraldic glass.

Kingsbury Episcopi c. 1450, heraldic glass and Passion symbols, north transept north window.

Kingstone 15th-century figures, north windows.

Langport c. 1490, figures of SS Cecilia, Elizabeth, Laurence, Anthony, Clement, Peter, Gregory, Joseph of Arimathea and Annunciation, with many smaller figures of saints in the tracery, east window.

Leigh-on-Mendip 15th-century Passion symbols, west window.

Long Ashton 15th-century heraldic glass, and figures of SS Laurence and Stephen, Coronation of the Virgin, etc., chancel windows.

Luccombe c. 1538, heraldic glass, south aisle, east window.

Mark c. 1495, figures of SS Laurence, Stephen, Philip, Matthew, James Great, Dorothy, John Baptist and Christ, Passion symbols and heraldic glass, north aisle west window.

Marston Bigot 15th-century Flemish and Rhenish glass, including Annunciation, Moses' Spies, Life of St Bernard, Jacob before Esau and Fountain of Life Crucifixion, east window.

Marston Magna 15th-century angels, and Chalice and Host, nave south and chancel north windows.

Mells Late-15th-century figures of SS Sitha, Agatha, Mary Magdalene, Apollonia, Margaret and Catherine, north aisle windows.

Middlezoy Early-16th-century figure of St Dorothy, south aisle window.

Moorlynch 15th-century angel; late-16th-century Flemish panels, chancel north-west window.

Mulcheney 15th-century figures of St Anne and the Virgin, angel, priest and heraldic glass, east window; 16th-century Flemish roundels, chancel north and south windows.

*Nettlecombe c.*1525, figures of SS George, Peter, Laurence and heraldic glass, Trevelyan Chapel north-east window.

North Cadbury 15th-century figures of SS Apollonia, John Evangelist, Barbara, Edmund, Luke, Giles, Edward Confessor, Etheldreda and Agnus Dei, west window.

Norton-sub-Hamdon Late-15th-century figures of SS Mary Magdalene, Catherine, Luke, John Evangelist, Dorothy, Virgin and Child, Apollonia, etc., north and south aisle windows.

Nynehead 15th-century figure of St Margaret, south aisle east window; late-16th-century heraldic glass, south aisle.

Oake 15th-century figures of SS Jerome, Ambrose or Augustine, Bartholomew, and Thomas, nave north window.

*Orchardleigh c.*1450, musical angels; *c.*1480, figure of abbot; *c.*1510, musical angels, east window; *c.*1445, figures of SS Matthias, Simon, Jude and Bartholomew, chancel north window; *c.*1445, figures of SS John Evangelist, Philip, Andrew, Matthew, chancel south window; *c.*1430, Trinity, restored, chancel north-west window; *c.*1445, figure of St Michael; *c.*1450, musical angels; *c.*1480, St Edward, west window.

*Pendomer c.*1455, figure of St James Great, angel, heraldic glass, east window.

Pilton Late-15th-century figure of Precentor of Wells, Thomas Overay, chancel south-east window; 15th-century seraphim, north aisle east window.

Pitcombe 15th-century angels and heraldic glass, west window.

Pitminster 15th-century figures including SS Catherine and Margaret, heraldic glass, north aisle east window.

Queen Camel 15th-century figure of donor, north aisle window.

*Saint Catherine c.*1490, Crucifixion with Virgin and Saints John and Peter, heavily restored, east window.

Seavington Saint Mary 15th-century figures of SS Mary Magdalene and Margaret.

Stratton-on-the-Fosse 15th-century figures of Apostles, north windows.

Swell 15th-century angel with heraldic shield, east window.

Taunton, Saint Mary Magdalene Late-14th-century heraldic glass, north aisle windows; 15th-century Annunciation, St Anne and Virgin, St Catherine and John the Baptist, clerestory windows; 16th-century Flemish roundel of Feast at Cana.

Tickenham 14th-century Crucifixion, south aisle window; 14th-century Christ in Majesty, south aisle east window; late-14th-century heraldic glass, north aisle windows.

Trull Late-15th-century figures of SS Michael and George, chancel south window; late-15th-century Crucifixion, restored, east window.

Wells Cathedral Nave south window: *c.*1380, figures of knights; nave north window: 15th-century Coronation of Virgin; south transept south window: 15th-century figures; south choir aisle: *c.*1320, Coronation of Virgin, Crucifixion, Virgin and Child and St Michael; St Catherine's Chapel: mid-16th-century French panels of life of St John; St John Baptist Chapel east window: 14th-century figure of Christ; choir east window: *c.*1339, Jesse Tree and Doom; north choir windows: *c.*1340, figures of saints; south choir windows: *c.*1340, figures of saints; north choir aisle window: *c.*1320, Crucifixion, and SS Michael and John the Baptist; St Stephen's Chapel: *c.*1320, Christ, Popes and angels; Lady Chapel north and south windows: *c.*1300, figures of saints and prophets;

Lady Chapel north-west window: *c*.1300–1310, fragments including figures of angels, rising souls, soldiers, etc.; Chapter House stairway west windows: *c*.1285, grisaille glass; Chapter House window tracery: *c*.1315, Doom; north transept east clerestory window: *c*.1507, Flemish or German panels.

West Camel 15th-century figures of SS Andrew, Peter, Paul and priest, pulpit window.

Weston Zoyland Early-16th-century heraldic glass, south transept east window.

West Pennard Late-15th-century figures of saints including SS Barbara and Dorothy and Coronation of the Virgin, north aisle east window.

Winscombe 15th-century Crucifixion, St Anthony and donors; Passion symbols, east window; 15th-century figures of St James the Great, bishop and archbishop, south aisle window; 15th-century figure of St Catherine, north aisle window.

Winsford 15th-century Virgin and Child, east window.

Yeovilton c.1470, heraldic glass, tower west window.

STAFFORDSHIRE

Barton-under-Needwood 16th-century Crucifixion in 19th-century east window.

Biddulph 16th-century Flemish panel, west window.

Blithfield 14th-century grisaille and heraldic glass, chancel windows; *c*. 1526, figures of donors, north window.

Blore c.1460, figures of Virgin and donors, chancel window.

Broughton 15th-century figures including donors, east window; 16th-century heraldic glass, chancel north window.

Bushbury Early-14th-century figures of Christ and donor, chancel south window.

Checkley Early-14th-century grisaille glass with figures of SS Nicholas, Thomas, Thomas à Becket, John, Margaret, Abraham and Isaac, martyrdom of St Thomas à Becket, penance of Henry II, east window; early-14th-century grisaille glass and figures of Virgin and Child and priest, chancel north window; early-14th-century grisaille glass and figures of Moses and St John, chancel south window; 15th-century roundels of Labours of the Months, chancel south window.

Church Leigh 13th-century figures of SS Laurence, Stephen, Giles, Virgin, Christ and archbishop; 14th-century Crucifixion; 14th-century heraldic glass, chancel windows.

Elford c.1525, Flemish panels, south aisle west window.

Hamstall Ridware 13th-century grisaille glass remains, north chapel window; 14th-century heraldic glass, south chapel.

Hanbury 15th-century Crucifixion, south aisle south-east window.

Lichfield Cathedral 1532–9, glass from Herckenrode Abbey, Belgium, in Lady Chapel windows. Seven large windows of Passion scenes, saints, donors and historical figures.

Okeover 14th-century donor figure, chancel window.

Seighford 15th-century Virgin and Child and St Christopher, chancel window.

Trysull Late-14th-century figures in east window.

Weston-under-Lizard 14th-century figures of donors and heraldic glass, east window.

Whittington 15th-century figures, very restored, chancel south window.

SUFFOLK

Bardwell c.1440, figures of donor knights and lady, with heraldic glass, nave north windows.

Barton Mills 14th-century figures including St John the Baptist, dragons, birds and heraldic glass.

Blythburgh 15th-century figures including St Felix, north and south aisle window tracery.

Bury St Edmunds, St James Early-16th-century Jesse Tree remains, and figures including St Catherine, Joachim, bishop, and angel.

Buxhall 14th-century figures of Christ, saint and angels, west window.

Combs 15th-century remains of Act of Mercy – giving drink to the thirsty and feeding the hungry, baptism, panels of the life of St Margaret; kings and patriarchs of Jesse Tree in tracery, south aisle window.

Denston 15th-century figure of knight and donor, east window.

Gazeley 15th-century figures of saints including St Apollonia, archbishop, angels, Passion symbols and heraldic glass, clerestory windows.

Gipping Late-15th-century figures of SS Mary and John, abbot, donor knight and lady, angels, east window.

Gislingham 14th-century Coronation of Virgin, Crucifixion and king, nave north and south windows.

*Great Bricet c.*1330, figures of the Evangelists, south window.

Great Saxham 16th-century foreign panels, west window.

Herringfleet 15th-century figures and Passion symbols, chancel windows.

Hessett 15th-century panels of St Nicholas, east window; 15th-century Resurrection, Scourging, etc., north aisle windows; 15th-century figure of St Paul and angels, south aisle windows; 15th-century musical angels and donor, tower window.

*Long Melford c.*1480, figures of Clopton family, friends and ancestors, with Saints Edmund, Gabriel, Raphael, Andrew, Peter Martyr and Dominic, and Pieta, with donors, north aisle windows; 15th-century Lily Crucifix, Clopton Chantry east window.

Lavenham 15th-century figure of Saint Giles.

Nowton 16th century, many Flemish medallions.

Risby 14th-century figures of saints and kings, chancel windows.

Sotterley 15th-century figures of Apostles and donors, east window.

Spexhall 15th-century heraldic glass.

Stonham Aspall 14th-century heraldic glass, clerestory windows.

Stratford, St Mary 15th-century figures and heraldic glass, north aisle west window.

Thorndon 16th-century Flemish medallions.

Ufford 15th-century Annunciation, chancel window tracery.

Yaxley 15th-century figures including Saint John, east window.

SURREY

Ashtead 16th-century Crucifixion, German, east window.

Buckland 14th-century figures of SS Peter and Paul; 15th-century Virgin and Child, nave north window.

Compton Mid-13th-century Virgin and Child, east window.

*Great Bookham c.*1500, seven Flemish panels.

Merstham 15th-century figures of Virgin and SS Peter and Catherine, south chancel aisle east window.

Mickleham Early-16th-century Flemish panel, vestry door window.

Oakwood c.1260, grisaille glass, chancel south window.

Ockham 15th-century angels, chancel south windows.

Oxted Mid-14th-century Evangelist's symbols, east window.

Pyrford Late-14th-century Trinity, east window.

Shere 13th-century grisaille glass and heraldic glass, chancel windows; 14th-century Evangelist's symbols and 16th-century heraldic glass, south chancel aisle east window.

Stoke d'Abernon 15th- and 16th-century English and Flemish glass, chancel windows; c.1510, Virgin, French; 15th-century English figures, nave windows.

Thorpe St Mary 16th-century Flemish medallions, north window.

Thursley 15th-century figures of saint and donor, Flemish.

West Horsley c.1220, martyrdom of St Catherine, Last Supper, grisaille glass, east window; c.1388, figure of knight, north window.

Wimbledon c.1365, figure of St George, Cecil chapel south window.

Worplesdon 14th-century figures of two saints, donors, north aisle window; late-15th-century priest, north window.

SUSSEX

Alfriston c.1360, figure of St Alphege, north transept window.

Battle c.1500, figures of bishops and archbishops, nave windows.

Bexhill 15th-century figures of saints and Coronation of Virgin.

Chalvington 14th-century figure of St Thomas à Becket.

Cowfold Late-13th-century Crucifixion.

Eastbourne, Saint Mary 15th-century Flemish panels, including Crucifixion, Solomon and Sheba and Prodigal Son, aisle east window.

Eastergate 15th-century heraldic glass.

Etchingham Late-14th-century heraldic glass.

Frant 15th-century figures, perhaps Flemish, north and south windows.

Hooe 15th-century figures of Edward III and Queen Philippa, Coronation of Virgin.

Linch 16th-century panels of Ascension and Deposition, Flemish.

Newick c.1315, Agnus Dei, chancel window.

North Stoke Early-14th-century Coronation of Virgin.

Pagham 16th-century French glass from Rouen.

Penhurst 15th-century heraldic glass.

Poynings 15th-century Annunciation, north transept east window.

Rodmell c.1500, Trinity, vestry window.

Shermanbury 15th-century figure of St Giles, west window.

Southover 15th-century figure of lady.

Stopham 15th-century heraldic glass.

Ticehurst 15th-century remains of Doom, with Virgin and Child, St Christopher and St Mary Salome with St John, chancel north window; 15th-century Coronation of Virgin, angels, etc., vestry window.

Tortington 14th-century Evangelist's symbols, east window.

Westham c.1420, figures of the Apostles, tracery of east window.

Wilmington 15th-century figure of· St Peter, possibly Flemish.

Woolbeding c.1500, Flemish glass.

WARWICKSHIRE

Arley Early-14th-century figures including Virgin and saints.

Avon Dasset 14th-century figure of bishop.

Baddesley Clinton Early-16th-century heraldic glass, east window.

Bilton 14th-century Crucifixion, 15th-century November from Labours of the Months, chancel north and north aisle east windows.

Caldecote 15th-century figure of saints, west window.

Castle Bromwich 15th-century figure of St Laurence, nave window.

Chadshunt 1558, Italian glass, north transept window.

Cherington Early-16th-century figures, nave north and south.

Coughton 15th-century figures of saints, east window.

Coventry, St Mary's Hall c.1500. Royal figures, north window.

Fillongley 15th-century figures of donors, north chapel window.

Haseley 15th-century panels of Annunciation, with SS Catherine and Winifred, and priest, west tower window.

Kinwarton 14th-century Virgin and Child, with donors, chancel south window.

Ladbroke 15th-century figures of SS Cuthbert, Chad and Giles, south-east window.

Leamington 15th-century figures, heavily restored and mixed with modern glass.

Lighthorne 15th-century figure of St Sebastian, south window.

Mancetter 1300–1350, remains of Jesse Tree, and SS Paul, Margaret, Bartholomew, John Baptist, James Great and angels, east window.

Merevale 14th-century Jesse Tree remains, 15th-century figures in tracery, east window.

Nether Whitacre Early-14th-century angel, chancel south window.

Packwood Early-14th-century Crucifixion, north transept window.

Preston-on-Stour Early-16th-century glass, west window; later foreign glass in chancel windows.

Quinton (near Pebworth) 14th-century Virgin, Lady Chapel window.

Stoke 15th-century heraldic glass.

Warwick, St Mary c.1447, figures of SS Thomas à Becket, Alban, Winifred, John of Bridlington and Elizabeth, with Virgin and donor Richard Beauchamp, Beauchamp chapel, east window; c.1447, musical angels, with words and music of the antiphon 'Gaudeamus' north and south window tracery, Beauchamp Chapel; c.1370, figures; c.1500, panels, vestry window.

Whichford 14th-century Crucifixion and Annunciation.

Wixford c.1400, heraldic glass, St John's Chapel east window.

Wolverton 14th-century remains of Doom and heraldic glass, east window; 14th-century figures of SS Anthony and Peter, angel and donor, nave north window.

Wooten Wawen 14th-century angels, east window.

Wroxall Abbey 15th-century figures of saints, east window.

WESTMORLAND

Beetham 15th-century figures in modern west window; 15th-century figure of a king, south chapel window.

Bowness Early-14th-century Virgin; later-15th-century Crucifixion, figures of SS George, Barbara, Catherine, Laurence and Stephen, with donors and heraldic glass, east window.

Brough 15th-century Crucifixion, figures of John the Baptist, a bishop and priests, north window.

Clifton 15th-century figures of Virgin and St John, east window.

WILTSHIRE

All Cannings 15th-century figure of Gabriel, south transept window.

Boyton 14th-century heraldic glass; 1484, Assumption and Annunciation, German; 15th-century figure of Christ.

Bremhill 15th-century figures of SS George, Aldhelm and Alfred, north aisle north-east window.

Broughton Gifford 15th-century figure of Virgin, with angels.

Crudwell 1450–80, Seven Sacraments subjects, north window.

Edington Priory 14th-century figures of SS William of York, Paul, Cuthbert, Audoenus and bishop, nave clerestory windows; 14th-century figures of Virgin and St John, north transept east window.

Lacock Abbey 15th-century Crucifixion and figure of St Erasmus.

Lydiard Tregoze 15th-century angels, nave, north and south windows.

Mere Late-14th-century figures of SS Nicholas, Martin, Christopher and archbishop, Bettesthorne Chapel, south windows; 14th-century pattern glass, north chapel window.

Mildenhall 15th-century figures including Saint Augustine, chancel windows.

Oaksey 15th-century figures of Virgin, Saint Anne and the Virgin, St Nicholas and donors, nave north window.

Purton 15th-century figures of SS Laurence and Stephen, nave north window.

Rushall 15th-century Crucifixion with Virgin and St John, and Virgin and Child, nave north window.

Salisbury Cathedral 13th-century grisaille glass, north and south aisle west windows; mid-13th-century Jesse Tree remains; *c.*1255, bishop and king; 13th-century Adoration of Magi, angels, etc., south nave window; 13th-century grisaille glass; 1270–80, heraldic glass; 13th-century medallion; 15th-century figures of SS Anthony and Peter; 16th-century Crucifixion, west window.

Steeple Ashton 15th-century coronation of the Virgin, south chapel east window.

Urchfont 14th-century angels, chancel windows.

Westwood 15th-century Lily Crucifixion, with Passion symbols, figures of SS Peter, Andrew, Michael and John the Baptist, with Virgin, chancel windows.

Wilton Early-13th-century French glass, medallions and figures.

Winterbourne Earls 13th-century medallions.

Yatesbury 15th-century Evangelist's symbols.

WORCESTERSHIRE

Abbotts Morton 15th-century heraldic glass, north transept north window.

Alfrick 16th-century Netherlandish glass

Ashton Underhill 15th-century heraldic glass.

Birts Morton Late-14th-century St Christopher, chancel south window.

Bredon Early-14th-century figures of SS Mary Magdalene and Mary of Egypt, 14th-century heraldic glass, chancel north window.

Cotheridge 15th-century heraldic glass, vestry window.

Doverdale 15th-century Virgin, very restored.

Droitwich, Saint Peter's Early-14th-century Crucifixion, Virgin and Pelican in Piety, south transept east window.

Eckington 15th-century figure of woman, chancel north window.

Evesham, All Saints 14th-century figure of Christ, north aisle window.

Fladbury 14th-century Virgin and Child, vestry window; early-15th-century heraldic glass, chancel north window.

Great Malvern Priory c.1485, twelve panels of life of Christ, nave north aisle window; 15th-century figures of saints, north aisle window tracery; c.1480, figures of saints and angels, west window; c.1501, 'Magnificat' window: panels of life of Christ, Coronation of Virgin, angels, saints, Passion symbols, Royal figures, north transept north window; c.1480, Last Supper, saints, north transept west window; 15th-century figures of angels, saints and Passion symbols, choir clerestory south windows; 15th-century life of St Wulstan, saints and life of Virgin, choir clerestory north windows; 15th-century life of Virgin, north choir aisle window; 15th-century, thirty-three panels of Creation, Adam and Eve, Noah and the ark, Abraham, Isaac and Jacob and Moses, south choir aisle windows; c.1440, fourteen panels of Passion subjects, c.1450, donor figures, musical angels, saints and Apostles in tracery, east window.

Grimley 15th-century Annunciation, God, St John, north and south windows.

Hampton Lovett 1561, heraldic glass.

Himbleton 13th-century medallion of St Mary Magdalene, east window; c.1400, Virgin and St John, Shell Chapel east window; 15th-century figures of SS John and George, north aisle windows; c.1450, figures of St Anne and the Virgin, SS Christopher and Catherine, chancel north window.

Holt 15th-century Annunciation, south chapel window.

Huddington Early-16th-century Crucifixion, much restored.

Inkberrow 15th-century figures of saints and angels, north aisle west window.

Kempsey 14th-century figures, chancel windows.

Little Malvern Priory c.1481, figures of Edward, Prince of Wales, and Queen Elizabeth Woodville, Christ and heraldic glass, east window.

Mamble c.1320, Crucifixion.

Oddingley c.1500, figures of SS Martin and Catherine, donors and heraldic glass, east window.

Queenhill Early-14th-century heraldic glass.

Warndon Early-14th-century Virgin, east window.

YORKSHIRE

Acaster Malbis c.1320, figures of Christ, SS Bartholomew, Peter, James Great, Alban and Julia, with heraldic glass, east window.

Almondbury 15th-century figures of SS Elizabeth, John Baptist, Helena, Barbara, St Anne and the Virgin, St Margaret, donors and heraldic glass, Kaye Chapel east and north windows.

Batley 14th-century Crucifixion and Virgin, south aisle window.

Beverley Minster 13th-century medallions and ornamental panels, with 14th-century pieces; 15th-century figures of saints and apostles, with angels, in upper lights and tracery, east window.

Bolton Abbey 14th-century heads and quarries, north aisle windows.

Bolton Percy c.1478, figures of SS John, Mary Magdalene, Agnes, Dorothy, Barbara, Helena, Margaret, Peter, Anne and the Virgin, Elizabeth, John the

Evangelist, Virgin and Child, with five archbishops and angels, east window; c.1478, Orders of Angels, chancel north and south window tracery.

Bradfield 15th-century figures of bishops and saints, north windows.

Coxwold 15th-century figures of angels and saints, north and south windows.

Darton 1526, figure of St Mary Magdalene, north chapel north window.

Dewsbury 14th-century grotesques, heraldic glass and early-15th-century roundels of Labours of the Months, north transept north window.

Ecclesfield 15th-century figures of donors and heraldic glass, north aisle window.

Elland 1481, ten panels of life of the Virgin, restored and with modern panels, east window.

Ellerton 14th-century heraldic glass, nave windows.

Emley 15th-century Crucifixion and figures of St George and donors, east window.

Folkton 14th-century figure of bishop and heraldic glass, nave north window.

Gilling 14th- and 15th-century glass in chancel north and south windows.

Grinton 15th-century figure of St George, east window.

Guisborough c.1500, figures of the Virgin and John the Baptist south aisle west window.

High Melton 14th-century figures of Virgin and Child and Archbishop Melton, south aisle west window; 15th-century remains of Doom and heraldic glass. north window; c.1400. Resurrected Christ, north window.

Hooton Roberts 15th-century figure of an archbishop, north window.

Hornby 14th-century grisaille glass, north aisle east window.

Kirkby Wharfe 15th-century foreign panels of life of Christ, and Abraham and Isaac, chancel windows.

Kirk Sundall Early-16th-century figures of St Margaret, bishop, etc.

Ledsham 15th-century figures of SS Catherine and Margaret, south nave window.

Methley 15th-century figures of SS Jerome, Ambrose, Margaret, Christopher, John the Evangelist, John Baptist, Augustine and Gregory, with angels and heraldic glass, Waterton Chapel windows.

Middleham 15th-century martyrdom of Saint Alkeda, north aisle west window.

Nether Poppleton 15th-century figures of saints, nave windows; 15th-century Coronation of the Virgin, chancel south window.

Normanton Late-15th-century Pieta with SS John and Mary Magdalene, east window.

Patricks Broughton 15th-century figures, north aisle west window.

Ripon Cathedral c.1320–30, medallion including SS Andrew, Paul and Peter, south aisle window.

Roos 15th-century angel, south clerestory window.

Ryther 14th-century figure of saint and heraldic glass, south aisle west and east windows.

Selby Abbey c.1340, Jesse Tree, much restored, with figures of saints and Doom in tracery, east window.

Sheffield Cathedral 14th-century remains of Jesse Tree.

Tadcaster 15th-century figures of St Catherine, bishop and donor.

Thirsk 15th-century figures of SS Leonard and Anne with Cleophas, and heraldic glass, south aisle east window.

Thornhill 1499, Jesse Tree, much restored, with saints in tracery, east window; c.1447, panels of the Three Holy Families, with donors, Saville Chapel south window; c.1493, panels of life of the Virgin, with SS George, Christopher,

Laurence and Stephen, Saville Chapel south-east window; 1493, Doom panels, Saville Chapel east window; 15th-century pieces including heads, south window; late-14th-century Crucifixion, and heraldic glass, Saville Chapel north window.

Thorpe Bassett 14th-century Crucifixion and heraldic glass, chancel windows.

Thrybergh 15th-century figures of Christ, musical angels and donors, west window.

Wales 15th-century figures of donors, nave north windows.

Wath Late-13th-century panel, chancel south window; 14th-century Crucifixion, transept south window.

*Well c.*1350, figure of knights of the Neville family, much restored, with heraldic glass.

West Tanfield 15th-century figures of SS John the Baptist, James Great, William, Michael, Ambrose and Virgin, and heraldic glass, north aisle window.

Wigginton 14th-century Crucifixion.

Winteringham 15th century, many figures of saints in aisle windows.

Woolley 15th-century Resurrected Christ and heraldic glass, north chapel north window; 15th-century figures of St George with donors and heraldic glass, north chapel north window; 15th-century Crucifixion, north chapel east window; 15th-century Virgin and Child, Trinity and Saint Catherine, south chapel east window.

Wycliffe Early-16th-century figures of Virgin and Child, Christ, Trinity and musical angels, south windows.

*York: All Saints, North Street c.*1430–40, figures of SS Thomas and William of York, and Christ, north aisle window; *c.*1440, Works of Mercy, with donors, north aisle window; early-15th-century 'Pricke of Conscience' subject, north aisle window; *c.*1330, Adoration of Magi, Annunciation, Crucifixion, Nativity, Coronation of Virgin and Resurrection, with figures of SS Michael and George and Virgin, north aisle east window; 1412–28, figures of SS John the Baptist, Anne and the Virgin, Christopher with Trinity and donors, east window; 14th-century Crucifixion, Gethsemane and donors, south aisle east window; *c.*1440, figures of SS Michael and John, south aisle south window; 15th-century Corpus Christi procession remains, south aisle south window; *c.*1440, figures of John the Baptist and Virgin and Child, with Mass of St Gregory, south aisle window.

*York: All Saints, Pavement c.*1370, eleven panels of Passion scenes, with Trinity, Coronation of the Virgin, Doom figures and 16th-century Flemish Crucifixion, west window.

York: St Denys 14th-century Jesse Tree remains, north aisle east window; 12th-century medallions and other 14th-century glass, north aisle north-west window; 15th-century figures, north aisle and south aisle windows.

York: Holy Trinity, Goodramgate 1470, figures of SS George, John Evangelist, Christopher, Ursula, Trinity, Holy Families, Risen Christ, east window; 15th-century figures of Coronation of Virgin, and Virgin and Child, north aisle east window; 15th-century heraldic glass, south windows.

York: St Helen 15th-century figures under 14th-century canopies, Coronation of Virgin, east window.

York: St Martin cum Gregory 14th-century figures including St Martin, and 15th-century donors, south aisle east window; 14th-century figures of SS John the Baptist and Catherine, north aisle window.

York: St Martin le Grand 15th century, thirteen panels of life of Saint Martin, with donors, west window; 15th century, many figures of saints, including SS George, Barbara and Holy Family, with the Trinity and heraldic glass, three south aisle windows; later-15th-century figures of SS Christopher, Barbara,

Catherine, Denys, Ambrose, Augustine, Jerome and Gregory, with donors, bishops and Evangelist's symbols, north clerestory windows.

York: St Mary Castlegate Early-14th-century figures of John the Baptist, king, etc., south aisle east window.

York: St Michael le Belfrey 1330, Annunciation, Nativity, Crucifixion, Resurrection, Coronation of the Virgin, with SS James the Great, Peter, Paul and Michael, murder of St Thomas à Becket, angels and heraldic glass, east window; *c.*1530, panels of story of adulterers, donors, north aisle north-east window; *c.*1535, figures of SS Ursula, Michael and Christopher, with Annunciation and donors, north aisle window; *c.*1537, figures of SS Christopher, Edward Confessor, Catherine and Thomas Didymus, with donors, north aisle north-west window; 1535, figures of SS James the Less, James the Great, Martin and Bishop, with donors, south aisle south-west window; *c.*1515, figures of SS George, Martin, Christopher and bishop, south aisle window; 1532, figures of SS Hugh, Paul, Peter and bishop, south aisle window; *c.*1535, figures of SS John the Baptist, Peter, James Great and bishop, with donors, south aisle south-east window.

York: St Michael, Spurriergate Mid-15th-century remains of Orders of Angels subject, south aisle south-east window; early-15th-century Jesse Tree remains, south aisle window; 15th-century figures including SS Ambrose, John Baptist and Micahel, south aisle window; 15th-century figures of God and Trinity, south aisle east window.

York Minster Mid-14th-century figures of apostles, saints, archbishops, Annunciation, Resurrection and Ascension, Coronation of the Virgin, west window; 1338, Crucifixion, with donor and saints in tracery, nave south aisle west window; 1338, figures of saints and panels of life of Virgin, nave south aisle, first window from west; 14th-century figures of saints and Annunciation, nave south aisle, second window from west; *c.*1310, Jesse Tree, restored, nave south aisle, third window from west; *c.*1315, Mauley family donors, much restored, and martyrdoms of SS Stephen, Andrew, John Baptist, nave south aisle, fourth window from west; early-14th-century life of St John, with donor, nave south aisle, fifth window from west; 14th-century Gospel scenes with donor, nave south aisle, sixth window from west; 14th-century life of St Nicholas, nave south aisle, seventh window from west; *c.*1150, panel from Jesse Tree; *c.*1330, panels of Annunciation, Nativity and Adoration of Magi, nave north aisle, second window from west; 14th-century 'Penitentiary' window, with martyrdoms of SS Peter and Paul, nave north aisle, third window from west; 14th-century 'Presentation' window, with martyrdoms of SS Denys, Laurence and Eleutherius and donor, nave north aisle, fourth window from west; *c.*1312, 'Pilgrimage' window, with Crucifixion, Saint Peter, donor and animal borders, nave north aisle, fifth window from west; *c.*1320, 'Bellfounders' window, with miracle of St William of York, and bell-founding scenes, north aisle, sixth window from west; *c.*1308, panels of life of St Catherine, with donor and heraldic figures in borders, nave north aisle, seventh window from west; 1422, St William of York window, 135 panels of life and miracles of St William, with donors, and archbishops, kings and angels in tracery, north choir aisle window; *c.*1445, St Cuthbert window, 104 panels of life and miracles of St Cuthbert, with Royal figures, archbishops and bishops, south choir aisle window; *c.*1385, Jesse Tree and Doom remains, south choir aisle; *c.*1410, Three Holy Families, south choir aisle window; *c.*1380, figures of SS James, John and Edward Confessor, and panels of life of Christ, south choir aisle window; *c.*1470, figures of Isaiah, King Edwyn, Trinity and angels, south choir aisle window; *c.*1420, crucifixion and martyrdom of St Stephen, with musical angels and Virgin and Child, north choir aisle east window; late-14th-century figures of SS Stephen, Christopher and Laurence, prophets, panels of life and Passion of

Christ, etc., three north choir aisle windows; c.1430, lives of Saints Chad and Paulinus, with donors and St Nicholas, north choir aisle window; c.1420, figures of SS John of Beverley, Thomas à Becket and William of York, north aisle window; 1405–8, 117 tracery panels of angels, patriarchs, prophets and saints, 117 main panels of Creation and Apocalypse, east window; c.1250, 'Five Sisters' grisaille glass windows, north transept north windows; c.1330, donors, late-15th-century donors, with Trinity and heraldic glass, 14th-century grisaille glass, life of John the Baptist, figures of saints, Coronation of Virgin, from St John's church, Micklegate, north transept windows; c.1307, six windows including lives of SS Catherine, Thomas of Canterbury, Christ, Peter and Paul, Chapter House windows; c.1310, many figures of saints, kings, bishops and prophets, vestibule windows.

Little medieval glass has survived in Wales or Scotland. In north Wales there are several important windows:

DENBIGHSHIRE
Gresford Late-15th-century life of the Virgin, ten panels, with donors, Lady Chapel east window; 1506–10, panels of martyrdom of John the Baptist and life of St Anthony, c.1500, figures of SS Apollonia, Christopher and Michael, south aisle chapel window; 1500, Jesse Tree in tracery, *Te Deum* in main lights, chancel east window.

*Llandyrnog c.*1480, remains of Seven Sacraments, with SS James the Great, John, Winifrid, Frideswide, Catherine, Asaph, and Annunciation.

Llanrhaidr 1533, Jesse Tree with twenty-two figures.

FLINTSHIRE
*Hope c.*1500, remains of *Te Deum* and Coronation of Virgin, nave windows.

Dyserth 16th-century Jesse Tree.

*Tryddyn c.*1350, figures of St Benedict and a knight.

In Scotland, the Burrell Collection in the Glasgow City Art Gallery, includes a considerable amount of English and foreign medieval glass.

Left : 'The Last Judgement',
detail, *c.* 1498 – Fairford,
Gloucestershire; *right :*
'Powers', from Nine Orders
of Angels, mid-fifteenth
century – choir north
clerestory, Great Malvern
Priory, Worcestershire

Left : 'The Annunciation', Flemish, *c.* 1510 – Marston Bigot, Somerset; *right :* 'St Martin', York school, *c.* 15 – St Michael le Belfrey, Yo

APPENDIX I: GLOSSARY

Annealing	The toughening of glass, by cooling it slowly after heating to a high temperature.
Boss	1. In glass, a disc of coloured or painted glass at the intersection of a geometrical design. 2. In masonry, a knob, usually carved or decorated, at the meeting point of ribs in a vaulted arch.
Byzantium	The ancient name for Constantinople, where, from the fourth century, a distinctive style of Christian art and architecture developed. By the ninth century its churches were richly decorated in paint and mosaic, and Byzantine art had considerable influence on the art and architecture of Europe, especially in the ninth and tenth centuries.
Canopy	The representation in glass of a hood or cover of the type used in architecture over niches, pulpits, doors and so on.
Cartoon	A full-size drawing on paper of the design for a stained-glass window, used by the glazier as a guide to its construction.
Censer	An incense burner, often shown carried by an angel.
Chancel	The east end of a church, where the altar is placed, usually separated from the nave by a screen or arch.
Chaplet	A band worn round the head, usually bearing a cross when worn by an angel.
Choir	In the larger church or cathedral, that part where the service is sung, between the nave and the altar.
Cinquefoil	A geometrical tracery form with five lobes.
Clerestory	The upper part of the main walls of a church, usually with a row of windows above the main ones.
Crocket	A leafy decoration used on spires, pinnacles, canopies, etc. especially in the fourteenth century.
Decorated	The architectural style in fashion from around 1290 until about 1380. It is characterised by elaborate window tracery in geometrical or flowing patterns, and naturalistic decoration.
Early English	The architectural style prevailing from around 1190 to about 1290, employing the pointed arch and lancet window.

Elevation	The representation of the vertical faces or surfaces of a building.
Finial	The leafy termination to a spire or canopy top.
Fleur-de-Lis	A stylised representation of a lily flower, used in the French Royal arms.
Galilee chapel	One placed at the west end of a church.
Gothic	A term used first to describe the style of architecture which employed the pointed arch. It came into use with the completion of the Church of St Denis, in France, and lasted until the sixteenth century. The term is also used to describe the art of the later Middle Ages.
Grotesque	A fanciful decoration, usually of a mythical beast or weird human figure.
Guild	A medieval organisation of craftsmen, having many of the functions of a trade union, or a religious society of laymen.
Iconoclast	A destroyer of holy images.
Jesse Tree	The literal representation of the family tree of Christ in glass. The figure of Jesse, founder of the House of David, lies at the bottom, and from him springs a vine or tree bearing Christ's ancestors in its branches.
Lancet	The narrow and pointed arched window of the Early English period, with the shape of the blade of a surgeon's knife.
Lights	The spaces or compartments between the stone framework of the window.
Mandorla	An almond-shaped radiance surrounding holy figures, notably the Virgin at her Assumption.
Mullions	The vertical bars of masonry in a window.
Nave	The main body of the church, at the western end, separated from the chancel by a screen or arch.
Nimbus	The halo surrounding the heads of holy figures. That of Christ always has a cross.
Ogee	A double curved shape like a shallow S. It was introduced in architecture around 1300 and was employed a great deal in the window tracery of the decorated period. The shape is reflected in the S-pose of figures in the glass of this time.
Paten	The plate used to hold the Host at Mass or communion.
Perpendicular	The architectural style in use from about 1380 until the middle of the sixteenth century. Windows were large, with parallel-sided tracery compartments made by continuing the vertical lines of the mullions of the main lights into the tracery.
Plan view	The representation of the horizontal surfaces of a building, drawn as if seen from directly above.
Putti	Small naked boys, or 'cupids', used as a decorative motif in Renaissance art.

Quatrefoil	A four-lobed geometrical tracery form.
Renaissance	In architecture, a style originating in Italy about 1420, and lasting until the middle of the sixteenth century. It was based upon a revival of classical Roman art. Its influences did not reach England much before the end of the fifteenth century, and are most apparent in glass painted by or under the influence of foreign glaziers, in the early sixteenth century.
Romanesque	The architectural style prevailing in the eleventh and twelfth centuries. It is characterised by the rounded arch and window head.
Sanctuary	The most holy part of the chancel, at the eastern end, surrounding the altar.
Tracery	The decorative apertures above the main lights of a window.
Transepts	The arms of a cross-shaped church, running north to south at right angles to the east-west orientation of the main building. Large churches may have two sets of transepts.
Trefoil	A three-lobed geometrical tracery compartment.
Triforium	A passageway around the walls of a large church, just below the clerestory. It is usually open to the body of the church, and may have its own windows.
Vanishing point perspective	The horizontal parallel lines of, say, a tiled floor are drawn so as to converge upon a distant point. It appears in glass of continental manufacture or influence from around 1500.
Vaulting	The ribs of an arched roof, ceiling or canopy.

APPENDIX II: BIBLIOGRAPHY

General books on English stained glass:

ARNOLD, HUGH. *Stained Glass of the Middle Ages in England and France* (Macmillan) 1913, reprinted 1956

BAKER, JOHN. *English Stained Glass of the Medieval Period* (Thames and Hudson) 1978

DAY, LEWIS. *Windows : A Book about Stained and Painted Glass* (Batsford) 1909

EDEN, F. SIDNEY. *Ancient Stained and Painted Glass* (Cambridge University Press) 1933

LE COUTEUR, J. D. *English Medieval Painted Glass* (Society for Promoting Christian Knowledge) 1926

LEE, L., SEDDON, G., STEPHENS, F. *Stained Glass* (Mitchell Beazley) 1976

NELSON, PHILIP. *Ancient Painted Glass in England 1170–1500* (Methuen) 1913

READ, HERBERT. *English Stained Glass* (Putnam) 1926

READ, HERBERT and BAKER, JOHN. *English Stained Glass* (Thames and Hudson) 1960

WESTLAKE, N. H. J. *History of Design in Painted Glass* (James Parker) 1879–94

WINSTON, CHARLES. *An Enquiry into the Difference of Style Observable in Ancient Glass Painting* (Parker, Oxford) 1847

WINSTON, CHARLES. *Memoirs Illustrative of the Art of Glasspainting* (John Murray) 1865

WOODFORDE, CHRISTOPHER. *English Stained and Painted Glass* (Oxford University Press) 1954

Books on particular areas or churches:

Cambridge:

HARRISON, K. P. *The Windows of King's College Chapel* (Cambridge University Press) 1952

JAMES, M. R. *A Guide to the Windows of King's College Chapel* (Cambridge University Press) 1899

Canterbury:

FARRAR, REV. F. W. *Notes on the Painted Glass at Canterbury* (Aberdeen University Press) 1897

HILL, REV. D. INGRAM. *The Stained Glass of Canterbury Cathedral* (Cathedral Guide)

RACKHAM, B. *The Stained Glass Windows of Canterbury Cathedral* (Society for Promoting Christian Knowledge) 1957

Fairford, Gloucestershire:

FARMER, O. G. *Fairford Church and its Stained Glass Windows* 1962

Great Malvern Priory, Worcestershire:

HAMAND, L. A. *The Ancient Windows of Great Malvern Priory Church* (Campfield Press) 1947

RUSHFORTH, G. MC. N. *Medieval Christian Imagery* (Oxford University Press) 1936

Norfolk:

WOODFORDE, CHRISTOPHER. *The Norwich School of Glasspainting in the Fifteenth Century* (Oxford University Press) 1950

Oxford:

GARROD, H. W. *Ancient Painted Glass at Merton College, Oxford* (Oxford University Press) 1931

GREENING LAMBORN, E. A. *The Armorial Glass of the Oxford Diocese 1250–1850* (Oxford University Press) 1949

HUTCHINSON, F. E. *Medieval Glass at All Souls College* (Faber and Faber) 1949

WOODFORDE, CHRISTOPHER. *The Stained Glass of New College, Oxford* (Oxford University Press) 1951

Somerset:

PEATLING, A. V. *Ancient Stained and Painted Glass in the Churches of Surrey* (Surrey Archaeological Society) 1930

ROBINSON, REV. J. ARMITAGE. *The Fourteenth-Century Glass at Wells* (Oxford) 1931

Surrey:
Winchester:
LE COUTEUR, J. D. *Ancient Glass in Winchester* (Warren and Sons) 1920

York:

HARRISON, CANON F. *The Painted Glass of York* (Society for Promoting Christian Knowledge) 1927

Books on stained glass in public collections:
Victoria and Albert Museum:
DAY, LEWIS F. *Stained Glass* (His Majesty's Stationery Office) 1913
RACKHAM, B. *A Guide to the Collections of Stained Glass* 1936

Leicester Museum:
Painted Glass from Leicester (Museum guide) 1962

Glasgow Art Gallery:
WELLS, WILLIAM. *Stained and Painted Heraldic Glass, Burrell Collection* (Gallery guide) 1962
WELLS, WILLIAM. *Stained and Painted Glass, Burrell Collection* (Gallery guide) 1965

The following are selected from the many books dealing with the content of medieval art:
Books on saints and their emblems:
CAXTON, W. (trans). *The Golden Legend* 7 vols. (J. M. Dent) 1931
FERGUSON, GEORGE. *Signs and Symbols in Christian Art* (Oxford University Press) 1961

MILBURN, R. C. P. *Saints and Their Emblems in English Churches* (Oxford University Press) 1949

ROEDER, HELEN. *Saints and Their Attributes* (Longmans, Green and Co.) 1955

General books on religious imagery:
ANDERSON, M. D. *Looking for History in British Churches* (John Murray) 1951

ANDERSON, M. D. *The Imagery of British Churches* (John Murray) 1955

MALE, EMIL. *The Gothic Image* (Collins Fontana Library) 1961

Books on costume and armour:
BLAIR, CLAUDE *European Armour* (Batsford) 1958

FAIRHOLT, F. W., revised by DILLON, H. A. *Costume in England* (George Hall) 1896

HOUSTON, M. G. *Medieval Costume in England and France* (Adam and Charles Black) 1939

WILLETT, C. and CUNNINGHAM, P. *Handbook of English Medieval Costume* (Faber and Faber) 1952

Books on Heraldry:
BOUTELL, C. *English Heraldry* (Gibbings and Co.) 1902

PINE, L. G. *Heraldry and Genealogy* (English University Press) 1957

PLANCHÉ, J. R. *The Pursuivant of Arms* (Chatto and Windus) 1851

SCOTT-GILES, C. WILFRED. *The Romance of Heraldry* (J. M. Dent) 1929

APPENDIX III: HOW TO PHOTOGRAPH STAINED GLASS

The photography of stained glass is straightforward enough in principle, but requires a little experience and some specialised apparatus if it is to be tackled successfully. While any format may be used, 35-mm cameras are recommended, since the range of equipment available is very wide, and the running costs, especially for colour, are much less than in most other systems. The single-lens reflex camera is ideal for the purpose, facilitating the accurate framing and focusing of the subject. Through-the-lens exposure measurement is available on a number of modern cameras; its advantages and disadvantages in stained-glass photography will be discussed later. The camera must be suitable for use with interchangeable lenses. When photographing stained glass, the principal difficulty will be getting close to the often small panels of glass so as to fill the frame, while at the same time photographing the glass from as near a right angle as possible to avoid distortion. On rare occasions the glass is at eye-level, and there will be no problem. Usually it is well above the normal eyeline. If no stepladder or scaffolding is available, and they are not usually to hand, the only solution will be to use a long-focus or tele-photo lens. Most of the photographs in this volume were taken with a lens of 300 mm focal length, the equivalent of a telescope magnifying six times. Had one been available, an even longer lens would have been useful on some occasions. A lens of intermediate focal length, say 135 mm, will cope with some of the larger, lower panels. The standard 50-mm lens is rarely of use except to record whole windows. Where it is possible to approach the window closely, extension tubes or close-up lenses may be needed to record very small details.

A firm tripod will be needed when using the long focal-length lenses. If the slower, high-definition colour films are used, exposure times may be for as long as six or twelve seconds at the smaller lens apertures. Any camera vibration will destroy the clarity of the photograph, since it will be magnified by the long lens. Some cameras have a range of slow speeds which can be triggered by the delayed-action mechanism normally used for self-portraits. This technique reduces the risk of camera-shake, set up when the release is pressed, since any such vibration has a chance to settle down before the shutter is released automatically.

Materials
Colour transparency film is the ideal material for recording stained glass. The reproduction is in essentially the same medium as the original, and should possess much of its brilliancy of colour when projected. The slower, high-definition films are to be preferred. High-speed colour films have no special advantage, since hand-held exposures are not desirable when the very long focal-length lenses are used. Once the camera has to be tripod mounted, the length of the exposure does not matter. Colour negative materials may be used when colour prints are more desirable, but no print on paper, however good, can match the effect of light

passing through a transparent medium. Black and white photographs of stained glass are generally so disappointing that they are not worth considering, except where details of line are all that is required.

Lighting conditions

For successful results, the window must be evenly illuminated *from the outside*. Flash on the camera is no use at all, although some people try it. A uniformly overcast grey sky, unsatisfactory for most colour work, is almost ideal for stained-glass photography. There will be no great variation in the illumination of windows in different parts of the church, nor of different areas within one window. The use of the ordinary skylight or UV filter recommended for general colour photography will counteract any slight tendency to blueness of colour cast under these conditions. Direct sunlight should be avoided. While it may produce a pretty play of colour within the church, it makes photography of the glass very difficult. Photographs made directly into the sun through the window will be very unevenly illuminated. Strong shadows of the usual protective grille or mesh outside the window will be thrown on the glass and confuse the detail. The same mesh, under the diffuse light of an overcast sky, will be almost invisible in the photograph. If the sun is low, the colour rendering may be distorted to give unacceptably warm results. Sunlight shining into a church can sometimes fall on the inside of a window to be photographed, lighting the leads and surrounding masonry and subduing the brilliance of the glass. It is not worth carrying on in such conditions. Wait until the sun moves on or goes in.

Windows are sometimes partly obscured by trees; wintertime may be better, when there is no foliage to obstruct the light. Nearby buildings may cast a shadow on the glass, and the diffuse light from an overcast sky may help reduce this problem. Alternatively, it may be necessary to photograph such a window from a more oblique angle, accepting the distortion in return for better illumination. Lamps, altar pieces and so on inside the church may pose similar problems.

Exposure

The determination of correct exposure is the key to successful stained-glass photography. In theory, those modern cameras with through-the-lens exposure measurement are ideal, but it is important to know whether the measurement is made over the whole field of view, or over a limited area of it. If the former, incorrect readings will be given when the field of view includes areas of greatly different brightness to the glass being photographed. A panel of old, dark glass surrounded by white glass would be such a case, where the meter, unduly influenced by the bright surround, would recommend an exposure too short for the coloured glass. If the meter reads over a limited (and known) area of the field, selective and more exact readings can be made. It is important to be able manually to adjust the camera or over-ride the exposure system of automatic cameras. Fully automatic cameras will often give incorrect results with these special subjects.

If a separate exposure meter is used the technique of measurement may have to vary with the circumstances. If the window can be reached, readings can be made directly on the glass. Holding the meter at a short distance from the window, an average reading will be given, adequate if the glass is of reasonably uniform density throughout the panel. A more accurate reading will be given by measuring the brightness of the darkest and lightest areas, and taking an exposure setting between the two. It may be necessary to favour the lighter or darker areas, depending upon their proportions in the window. In certain cases, especially in early windows, the range of brightness between the lightest and darkest glass will be too great for the film to record successfully, and a compromise must be made, based upon the method just described.

It is not, however, always possible to reach the window directly. If it is very large, an average reading may still be possible, provided that the window more than fills the angle of acceptance of the meter. Most meter manufacturers should give this information in their instructional literature, and it is desirable to know what it is. If the meter has a wide angle of acceptance it may include much of the dark surround to a window, giving a recommendation which would overexpose the glass in the photograph. The performance of the meter used should be understood so that suitable adjustments can be made to the exposure. If in doubt, and the church cannot be revisited, a range of exposures above and below the calculated one should be made to ensure at least one acceptable result.

Even if the glass is too far away to make an average reading there are ways in which an exposure estimation can be made. Another window with the same aspect and illumination may be more accessible, and readings made on this will give a guide to the exposure required. Of course, you must be sure that the two windows have glass of comparable density, but this is usually easily decided if they can be viewed from the same standpoint. If the glass to be photographed appears significantly darker or lighter than that used for the test reading, the exposure can be adjusted accordingly. Another technique used with success by the author is to go outside the church, to a point below the window which is to be photographed. If the meter used has an incident light attachment, the light falling on the window can be measured. With an average glass window, at least of the later periods, the light *passing through* the glass is comparable with the light *reflected from* an average subject, and the incident light reading will be a good guide to the correct exposure. Remember that if the window is predominantly dark or light, the exposure will need to be adjusted accordingly. If no incident light attachment is available for your meter, a normal reflected light reading may be made on a suitable subject nearby – the wall of the church (if it is not too light), grass under the window, or on a piece of medium-grey card carried in the camera case for this purpose. An experimental exposure range based upon a reading using such a piece of card would reveal what adjustment was necessary for future work, and would soon repay the small cost of the materials used.

Colour rendering
The colour of any object is not absolute, but is determined by the light falling on it. The colour of a stained-glass window will vary considerably at different times of the day, in different weather conditions and at different times of the year. A window lit by blue sky light in the morning will look very different when the late afternoon sun falls on it. Trees in leaf in spring or summer may reflect green light onto a window, with a result quite different from that when the trees are bare. Although these and other sources of variation constantly affect the colour of the window, the observer adjusts to them as the eye adapts to the overall colour changes. Colour films cannot adapt in this way, and such differences in the colour of the lighting are likely to be more visible on the film than to the eye. However, provided extremes are avoided – late sunlight is the worst offender – the majority of photographs should be perfectly acceptable. But remember that if you revisit a church to photograph the glass again it may not be possible to match the colour rendering of the earlier photographs, if the lighting conditions have changed.

Behaviour
While it should not be necessary to state it, the reader is reminded that parish churches are places of worship, and should be respected as such. Permission should always be sought *before* photographing in cathedrals or churches. Such permission will always be given if the request is made in a reasonable way and at a reasonable time. No furnishings should be moved in the church without express

authority. Never climb on tombchests, seats or altars to get your picture. That such behaviour is not uncommon is one of the reasons why many churches are now locked and why photography may not be permitted. A contribution to the fabric fund may help to ensure that future generations can enjoy and record the beauties of medieval glass.

INDEX

Acknowledgements
The courtesy and help of countless clergymen, vergers and churchwardens all over the country is gratefully acknowledged. The author's requests for permission to photograph the old glass in their charge were invariably met with the kindest and fullest co-operation. The advice and encouragement of Mr B. E. C. Howarth-Loomes during the preparation of the book was of great help.

DATE DUE